Live Move Grow

Preschool Curriculum

———

Brooke Neilson and Emily Shill

LIVE MOVE GROW PRESCHOOL CURRICULUM
©Copyright 2015 Live Move Grow

All Rights Reserved.
No part of this book may be reproduced,
scanned, or distributed in any printed or
electronic form without permission.

For Clark and Eli

Special thanks to:

Paige Batty—for her countless contributions to this curriculum
Laura Harper—for writing and performing her original composition, our Live Move Grow theme
Carter and Mason and their mothers, Paige and Jen—for experimenting with us
Lisa Fink and Teresa Anderson—for their professional advice and contributions
Jon Harper—for all of his technical support
Liza Dailey—for consultations and content editing
Jess Larsen—our editor, for making our vision marketable
Van Hansen—our CFO and business investor
David Anderson—our attorney
All of our test groups for their faith in us and feedback!

And most of all, to Mike and Otto for helping this dream become reality!

Table of Contents

Welcome Letter   1

Introduction   3

1. I Am Special   9

Unit 1: Exploring Our Senses

2. Sense of Sight   14
3. Sense of Hearing   18
4. Sense of Smell   24
5. Sense of Taste   30
6. Sense of Touch   37

UNIT 2: Things That Are Alive

7. Farm Animals   43
8. Wild Animals   50
9. Ocean Animals   57
10. Bugs   65
11. Reptiles and Amphibians   72
12. Birds   80

Thanksgiving Break

13. You Are Alive—Parts of the Body   88
14. You Are Alive—My Healthy Body   95

Unit 3: Things That Work

15. Safety   101

Christmas/New Years Break

16. Things That Work around the House   109
17. Things That Work outside the House   114
18. Music and Instruments   120
19. You Work—I Can Help at Home   127
20. You Work—Occupations   134

Unit 4: Things That Move

21. Occupational Vehicles   139
22. Cars, Trucks, and Automobiles   144
23. Planes, Trains, and Boats   149
24. Forces of Nature   156

25. Solar System 162
26. You Move—I Can Hike and Play 168
27. You Move—I Can Play Sports and Games 172

Take off one week in this unit for a spring break

Unit 5: Things That Grow

28. Types of Plants 175
29. How Plants Grow 180
30. Leaves 187
31. Trees 192
32. Flowers 198
33. Foods That Grow 204
34. You Grow 210

Appendices

Appendix A: Attention Grabbers 214
Appendix B: Free Play Ideas 215
Appendix C: Song lyrics & Sheet music 217
Appendix D: Lesson Images 221

Welcome to Live Move Grow™! We are thrilled to have you join us in this process of discovery and learning.

Through our research, we have learned that young children need less sitting and more moving. They need less classroom and more creativity. They need less quizzing and more inspiring. They need less pressure and more play. In short, they need fresh air and sunshine. They need to climb, touch, see, smell, hear, explore, and imagine. They need self-esteem and a healthy awareness of their own strengths and abilities. They need parents who are invested in their educational process from an early age. They need to develop a love of learning.

We also believe that preschoolers can develop fundamental life skills that will set them up for success later in their academic careers and lives. The following are some examples of the skills we have chosen to integrate into this curriculum along with a few of our reasons for doing so.

- *Attention span.* While focused mainly on moving and exploring, this curriculum incorporates just the right amount of storytelling, singing, and taking turns to begin increasing attention spans and preparing for formal school settings in later years.
- *Creativity and imaginative play.* We believe in teaching children to think outside of the box. Through encouraging their creativity and imagination, we teach them that they are unique individuals with bright minds and endless potential.
- *Critical thinking and problem solving.* We instill confidence within children by teaching them that they are capable of finding their own solutions.
- *Fine motor skills.* This essential piece of development prepares children for writing.
- *Curiosity.* We want to encourage children to see learning as an exciting and desirable process.
- *Gratitude.* Gratitude not only encourages kindness, respect, and fulfillment, but also discourages a sense of entitlement.
- *Gross motor skills.* Balance, coordination, and physical activity have been proven to be some of the most important pieces to a young child's physical, emotional, and mental development.
- *Patience and taking turns.* Children can learn the important skills of discipline and self-control.
- *Responsibility.* Children find great fulfillment when they complete an age-appropriate task and see the results of their work.
- *Sensory learning.* Using their senses helps children make connections in their minds through experience.
- *Sorting and puzzles.* These proven, powerful tools build parts of the brain that help children develop math skills.
- *Teamwork.* We want children to learn to work with others and be part of a team. Working together instills a responsibility to help others and appreciate their efforts.
- *Visual tracking.* This skill aids in cognitive development and prepares children for reading.

We wrote this curriculum to inspire parents and children everywhere. We wrote it for parents who long to teach, inspire, encourage and nurture the bright little minds and spirits under their care. We wrote it for parents and caregivers who want to foster within their children the skills and values that will assist them in finding their own happiness and success.

We wrote this for all the children with bright lights of excitement and wonder still in their eyes. We wrote this for children who want more chances to run and climb, more reasons to rise to new challenges, more opportunities to discover and explore, and more places to feel loved and encouraged.

Most of all, we wrote this for Eli and Clark, our inspirations and very reasons for living, moving, and growing.

May this curriculum re-inspire you to "un-plug" with your family and find together that learning is a wonderful process of discovery that never has to end.

All the best—

Brooke Neilson and Emily Shill
Founders of Live Move Grow™

Introduction

How To Be Successful with This Curriculum

Adapt to the needs of your group. Recognize that each group will have different attention spans, levels of skill and understanding, and unique strengths and weaknesses. We as writers cannot possibly cater to all situations, so use these outlines as a guide, and then remain sensitive to your group's needs as you decide where to cut out material and where to add or embellish. It is your responsibility as a teacher to adapt these lessons to your group's needs. (As a side note, we developed this curriculum to work equally well for boys and girls. In keeping with that vision, we have switched the gendered pronouns every other chapter, so odd chapters refer to a child as "he," and even chapters refer to a child as "she.")

Set realistic expectations. Please remember that you are working with three- to five-year-old children who are just beginning to learn the content and skills you are working to implement. Some lessons will go wonderfully, and the children will engage and participate in ways you didn't know they were capable of doing! There may be other weeks, however, when nothing goes according to plan, and your hard work and preparation appear to go unappreciated or feel useless. Know that this is not only normal but to be expected; the children are still learning in their own way. Some weeks your lesson will be short, and the children will spend more time in free play than they do in the lesson itself. Understand the important role that free play has in their development (and in this curriculum), and do not count this as a failure. Do not give up at the first sign of difficulty; while still recognizing that you can adapt when needed, it is important to continue to challenge them as they develop the ability to pay attention and participate. You will often be surprised how much they have retained when all is said and done!

Promote parent creativity. This curriculum is designed to not only enhance your child's learning experience but also to train parents as the primary teachers of their children. Use this curriculum as both a resource for teaching and an opportunity to come up with your own ideas that will aid your child in exploring and discovering the world around her!

Review the curriculum objectives. Understand that this curriculum's many objectives focus around researched-based needs of preschool-aged children. Because it's easy to focus on content rather than experience, implementing Live Move Grow objectives may at times feel counterintuitive. Review this list throughout the year to remind yourself of the following important goals:

1. **Experience:** Experience is more important than content! Always sacrifice content, when necessary, to enhance the experience for the child. If the child is excited about one portion of the lesson and disinterested about the next set of facts provided, feel free to spend more time on the area that your child is showing interest in and skip some of the other portions. Your natural tendency will be to get through material, but always remember to focus more on the experience, regardless of how much content is covered.

Children's sense of discovery and desire to explore will be enhanced, not squandered, as you listen to their interests instead of insisting on an agenda.

2. **Movement:** Movement is an integral part of this curriculum. It helps children's minds to engage while developing essential gross motor skills, balance, and coordination, which are important pieces to their development physically, mentally, and emotionally. We intentionally integrated movement frequently throughout this curriculum—embrace movement and practice as much as possible!

3. **Self-esteem:** This is one of the most important qualities a child can learn. Many of our activities center around building confidence in the children and encouraging them to explore their unique strengths, talents, opinions, and abilities to imagine and create. These skills will serve as fundamental building blocks of success as they continue academically in later years.

4. **Balance:** Strive to find the right balance between catering to needs and challenging abilities. Sometimes parents tend to assume that children are not capable of listening, trying new activities, or learning new skills or concepts. We purposely designed this curriculum to be enjoyably challenging for young children and to increase their abilities in many areas. Frequently introducing new vocabulary words is one way that we challenge the children throughout this curriculum, and we encourage you as teachers to embrace this! (For your convenience, we designate new words by italicizing them and putting an asterisk before them, e.g., *metamorphosis.*)

5. **Repetition:** Recognize that repetition can be a useful teaching tool. If you feel that there is too much of any given activity, skill practice, outing setting, or supplemental activity, ask yourself if the repetition of this activity can serve as a valuable teaching tool for your child.

6. **Enjoy:** This curriculum was written to be enjoyable and fun! Use it as a unique way to bond with your child as you learn and discover life together. Above all, have fun and love your child!

Utilize the teacher tips. A teaching tip is provided at the beginning of each lesson. Each tip is specific to the corresponding lesson but applicable throughout the entire curriculum. As such, the teacher tips serve as a valuable training resource for parents throughout the year, and we strongly recommend that all participating parents read each week's teaching tip (even for the weeks that they aren't teaching) and apply these principles whenever appropriate.

Review every lesson. In order to maximize the experience for the children, we recommend that parents read through every lesson, even the ones they do not teach. Armed with an awareness of the weekly content the children are learning about, parents will be more capable of initiating discussions, asking questions, replicating activities, and encouraging curiosity and discovery.

Plan ahead. Be sure to plan at least a week ahead, so you can check out books, reserve supplies, coordinate with parents, and get to know the lesson well. Ideally, a teacher should be able to teach a whole lesson without reading anything verbatim. This will leave you more freedom to focus on the children and their needs, rather than reading from the book. The outline page of each lesson plan contains most of what you will need for the entire lesson.

Participate. This curriculum was designed for parents who want to facilitate the best learning environment possible for their children. Recognize that while we have done our best to create exciting, stimulating, and meaningful lesson plans and outings, the majority of learning happens in your homes outside of the four hours Live Move Grow offers. In order to take full advantage of what this curriculum has to offer, attend outings every week with your child, spend time each week reading together from the book list, and utilize the activity and discussion portions of the parental supplement so you and your child can learn and grow together!

How to Get Started

Set up a group. An ideal size for a Live Move Grow preschool group is four to six children ages three and up. If your group differs from this structure, you may need to adapt this curriculum to meet your group's needs. When searching for group participants, consider that your greatest success in this curriculum will be found with parents who are interested in being heavily involved in their children's learning process. (Parents who simply want to teach their children on their own, without creating a group, can also use this curriculum successfully.)

Set up a parents' meeting. Before holding your first lesson, meet together with all of the participating parents to introduce the curriculum objectives, review the designated format, and establish rules unique to your group. Here is a sample outline for the meeting:

1. Review curriculum objectives.
    a. Encouraging movement and hands-on discovery
    b. Parental involvement in learning
    c. Fostering a love of learning and encouraging natural curiosity
    d. Teaching life skills and values

2. Discuss preschool format
    a. Determine which two days of the week and what time your group will meet. Every week, day one is an in-home lesson and day two is an outing that requires more parents to be present.

b. Reinforce that parents are responsible for the drop-off and pick-up of their children from all lessons. Parents are strongly encouraged to attend all outings.
c. Divide the teaching schedule between parents. Remind parents that the week they teach, they are also responsible for setting up the details of that week's outing and transferring the materials bin to the next teaching parents.

3. Suggested Items to Enhance your LMG Experience
   a. Carpets/Mats: Each child has her own carpet to sit on for the applicable lesson portions.
   b. Name tags: Each child should have a personalized name tag that you can use to assign carpets. This is also a basic introduction to recognizing their name in print.
   c. Walking rope: To use anytime you go outside during a lesson as a way to keep the group contained and safe.
   d. Music: The Live Move Grow Suggested Music List is a compilation of songs that can be used for welcome music and in individual lessons throughout the curriculum. It includes the Live Move Grow original theme song (sheet music is found in Appendix C).
   e. Curriculum Manual: Most parents find it helpful to have their own manual, for the parental supplement each week, and to prepare lessons ahead of time. How many manuals you purchase as a group is up to you.
   f. Calendar: A magnetic calendar can be used each week as a basic introduction to identifying days of the week, months of the year, seasons, holidays, and more.

4. Review the lesson format (as explained in the large heading below). Ensure that all participating parents are familiar with the lesson format.

5. Establish rules
   a. Discuss with the other parents how you will handle discipline issues when other parents are not present.
   b. Establish simple classroom rules for the group. Review them often with the preschoolers.

Lesson Format (total time typically 1.5–2 hours)

Welcome music/gather to carpets (5–10 minutes): While the children are arriving, use the Live Move Grow playlist as welcoming music, and encourage the children to sing and dance to the songs with you. Moving will aid their ability to concentrate on the lesson.

Welcome song (2 minutes): After the welcome music, you will officially begin each lesson with "The More We Get Together". See Appendix C for lyrics and instructions.

Attention grabber (2 minutes): Attention grabbers should be used between activities or any time the teacher needs to regain control and direct attention back to the lesson. We have purposefully provided only six options for this curriculum, which allows the children to become familiar with them and know that we are asking them to pay attention when we use them! Introduce the attention grabber of the day at the beginning of each week's lesson, and then use that same attention grabber throughout the lesson when needed. See Appendix A for a list of attention grabbers.

Calendar time (5 minutes): Using the calendar in the suggested LMG materials, or one of your own, and have the children take turns moving the magnets around on the board. Catering to attention spans, allow the children to help determine some of the following:

> Day of the week
> Month, date, year
> Weather
> Season
> Events, activities, and holidays
> Emotions
>
> When discussing the day of the week, sing the following to the tune of "Oh My Darling, Clementine":
>
> "There are seven days,
> There are seven days,
> There are seven days in a week.
> Sunday, Monday,
> Tuesday, Wednesday,
> Thursday, Friday, Saturday."
> (Repeat once)

Story time (5–10 minutes): The book for story time should be available at local libraries. The teacher is responsible for checking the book out or having it available during class. If you can't find the suggested story time book, try a different book from the Parental Supplement booklist. Encourage the children to sit quietly on their mats and listen to story time each week. Keep children engaged by showing pictures frequently and asking critical-thinking questions.

Transition activity (5–10 minutes): These activities will focus on movement, lesson content, or a combination of the two. They should serve as an opportunity for movement between the story time and lesson, which will then enhance the children's attention spans and ability to internalize the lesson content. Spend as much time with these activities as the children would like.

Lesson (15–30 minutes): The goal of the lesson portion is to challenge the children with new concepts and attention-span requirements, while incorporating skill objectives and encouraging movement, curiosity, and love of learning.

Hands-on activity (10–20 minutes): This section serves as a continuation of the lesson content while typically incorporating fine and gross motor skills, sensory development, and more freedom with expression and creativity.

Theme song (2 minutes): "Come Discover, Come Explore" (#2 on the LMG SUGGESTED SONG LIST) is the Live Move Grow theme song. Play it to conclude each week's lesson.

Children dismissed for free play (15–45 minutes): Free play is an integral part of this curriculum and will take place at the conclusion of every lesson. It is an essential component to healthy development because it encourages the use of imagination, helps children explore their independence, and teaches children positive social interaction skills.

Outing: Each week has a suggested outing as well as alternative options to accommodate most areas and climates. Parents should attend with their child.

Parental supplement: The weekly supplement contains books, activities, and discussion ideas. These correlate to the lesson topic and can be used by parents to continue discovering and learning with their child at home.

Lesson 1: You Are Special

Lesson Objective: Practice appropriate behavior for a preschool setting while also encouraging parents and children to work together.

Lesson 1 Skill Objectives:
- Attention span
- Critical thinking
- Decision making
- Emotional awareness
- Following directions
- Gross motor
- Listening
- Patience
- Receptive language
- Rhyming
- Self-esteem
- Taking turns

Preparation

Lesson Materials:
- Ask a parent to take photos of arriving children

Hands-on Activity Materials:
- Board or measuring tape

Parental responsibility:
- Help child bring one or two that are special to or represent that child
- Help child pick and answer one of the questions in the lesson (see step 1 of the lesson portion)
- Attend the first lesson

Lesson 1 Outline

1. Welcome music/gather to carpets

2. Welcome song: "The More We Get Together"

3. Attention grabber: One, Two, Three, Now Follow Me!
   Skills: attention span, following directions, listening

4. Calendar time
   Skills: patience, taking turns

5. Story time: *You Are Special* by Max Lucado (for this first lesson, consider reading the board book version of this story, which is shorter/simplified and may be more suited for their attention spans at this time)
   Skill: attention span, critical thinking, emotional awareness

6. Transition activity: Roll Call Activity
   Skills: critical thinking, following directions, gross motor, listening, receptive language, rhyming

7. Lesson: All about You
   Skills: decision making, emotional awareness, self-esteem,

8. Hands-on activity: How Tall Are You?
   Skills: taking turns

9. Theme song

10. Children dismissed for free play

Lesson 1 Details

Teacher Tip: Read the Introduction

It is essential to the success of this curriculum that each teacher/parent read through the Introduction.

Welcome Music/Gather to Carpets

Ask **a parent to take photos** of each child as he arrives. These pictures will be saved throughout the year and used in Lesson 34: "You Grow." Also take photos of each child with his accompanying parent or caregiver as a way to celebrate and acknowledge those relationships. (These photos can be e-mailed, printed, or otherwise distributed to the children.) After the photos are taken, each parent can lead his or her child to the individual carpet (or mat) with the child's name on it, where the child can dance or play to the welcome music. (For this first lesson, parents are welcome to stay with their children for the duration of the lesson.)

Transition Activity: Roll Call Activity

Skills: critical thinking, following directions, gross motor, listening, receptive language, rhyming

Get the children moving using the examples provided or several of your own. Repeat until you have given each child a command, and repeat with more commands if necessary to get wiggles out, regain attention, and prepare for the next activity. (Ex: Will a child whose name sounds like "Zarlie" jump in the air? [Charlie] Will a child whose name sounds like "Rofie" hop on one foot? [Sophie] Will a child who is wearing a blue shirt crawl to the table? Will a child who is wearing a red headband march to the couch? Will all the children with blue eyes do a summersault?)

Lesson: All about You

Skills: decision making, emotional awareness, self-esteem,

1. Before the lesson, tell the parents to help the children bring **one or two items that are special to them or represent them**. (If an item isn't applicable, the parent could bring a picture, share a song, demonstrate a talent, etc.) Also have the parents **help the children pick and answer one of the questions below**. (It is important that each parent allows the child to pick the question he wants to answer ahead of time. This promotes self-esteem and decision making and also allows the preschooler to pick what he is

comfortable answering.) Encourage parents to have their child practice this answer several times so he is comfortable sharing it with the class.
   a. What is something that makes you happy?
   b. What do you love to do?
   c. What does mom/dad love about you?
   d. What is something you're good at?

2. Begin the lesson by talking about what it means to be special. Discuss how each of us are *unique* (new word) with different strengths, likes/dislikes, physical features, etc. Explain, "These characteristics make us different from anyone else, and there is no one else exactly like you. Today we are going to learn about what makes each one of you special!"

3. Have Show and Tell using the items the children brought. Allow each child to share as much as he is willing on his own (parents can help when needed). Allow each child to have a turn.

4. Next, have a parent share a few unique things that make his or her child special. (This is an important opportunity to build the child's self-esteem.) Have the parent's child answer the pre-planned question (see step 1); this allows the child to take responsibility for identifying something unique about himself. Allow every parent and child to have a turn.

5. Encourage the other children to stay engaged and support each other by cheering and clapping for each other's answers. We recommend that parents pay attention too so they can better know the names and interests of the children they'll be teaching!

Hands-on Activity: How Tall Are You?

Skills: taking turns

Measure each child's height by marking a **board or measuring tape**. You will use this board or measuring tape again in Lesson 34: "You Grow." At that time you will measure the children and compare the measurements to show them how much they have grown throughout the year.

Lesson 1 Outing and Parental Supplement

Outing: None

No outing will be held during week 1. It is an orientation and welcome week.

Parental Supplement

Books:

- *ABC I Like Me!* by Nancy Carlson
- *I Like Me!* by Nancy Carlson
- *I'm 3! Look What I Can Do* by Maria Carluccio
- *You Are Special* by Max Lucado
- *Cloudette* by Tom Lichtenheld
- *It's Not Easy Being a Bunny* by Marilyn Sadler

Activities:

- Look in the mirror and talk nicely about yourself and others.
- Practice songs or activities introduced in Lesson 1.
- In your family, take turns sharing what you like and appreciate about each other.

Discussion:

- Discuss some of your child's talents and favorite things to do.
- How can we help make others feel special? What are some things you appreciate about other people, and how could you show them that appreciation?
- Talk about emotions and how some events of his day made him feel. Did he handle his emotions properly?
- Review friends' names from preschool.
- Review the preschool classroom rules that were established at the parents' meeting (see the introduction).

Unit 1: Exploring Our Senses
Lesson 2: Sense of Sight

Lesson Objective: Learn more about the sense of sight and practice using imagination.

Lesson 2 Skill Objectives:

- Creativity
- Critical thinking
- Fine motor
- Following directions
- Gross motor
- Imaginative play
- Patience
- Resourcefulness
- Sensory development
- Social-emotional development
- Taking turns
- Visual tracking

Preparation

Transition Activity Materials:

- Magic wand

Lesson Materials:

- Walking rope

Hands-on Activity Materials:

- Coloring materials
- Decorating materials (paint, stickers, etc.)
- Stapler or tape
- Scissors or hole punch
- Yarn or string

Parent Responsibility:

- Two empty toilet paper rolls or one paper towel roll cut into two even lengths

Lesson 2 Outline

1. Welcome music/gather to carpets

2. Welcome song: "The More We Get Together"

3. Attention grabber: Hocus Pocus, Everybody Focus!
   Skill: visual tracking

4. Calendar time
   Skills: patience, taking turns

5. Story time: *Brown Bear, Brown Bear, What Do You See?* by Bill Martin Jr.
   Skills: critical thinking

6. Transition activity: I Spy
   Skills: following directions, gross motor

7. Lesson: Sense of Sight
   Skills: gross motor, imaginative play, sensory development

8. Hands-on activity: Homemade Binoculars
   Skills: creativity, fine motor, resourcefulness

9. Theme song

10. Children dismissed for free play

Lesson 2 Details

Teacher Tip: Foster Imagination

Set the example when it's time to pretend. In this lesson, enjoy the fun, silly moments when you imagine with the children. Ask questions about what they "see" as they pretend to ride in a car or a plane, and encourage them to act out what they are doing. Imagining comes naturally to preschool-aged children, and it should be practiced, encouraged, and praised as often as possible. Using imagination is not just a healthy, important milestone for this age group—if encouraged, it will be an asset in many facets of their lives as they continue to grow.

Transition Activity: I Spy

Skills: following directions, gross motor

Pick an object around the room and describe its size, color, purpose, etc. Have the children guess and then run to that object. They can take turns using the magic wand (from the attention grabber) to point or tap the object. Repeat until everyone has had a turn.

Lesson: Sense of Sight

Skills: gross motor, imaginative play, sensory development

1. Discuss what our eyes can do (look, blink, wink, squint, close to sleep, etc.).

2. Explain what it means to use your imagination and how it is different from seeing.

3. Have the children *imagine* they are riding in the car. Allow them to move about the room on their "road trip." Occasionally, freeze and ask them what they imagine they see. (Ex: car seats, other cars, or street signs.)

4. Pretend to be on an airplane and have the children pretend to fly around the room. What do they see? (Ex: sky, birds, clouds, lightning, the city below, or other planes.)

5. Use the walking rope to have the children pretend they are walking around the park. What do they see? (Ex: trees, playgrounds, or birds.)

Hands-on Activity: Homemade Binoculars

Skills: creativity, fine motor, resourcefulness

Each child should bring two empty **toilet paper rolls** or one **paper towel roll** cut into two lengths. Have the children decorate their tubes using **coloring** or **decorating materials** (like paint or stickers). Help them assemble the binoculars using a **stapler** or **tape**. Using **scissors** or a **hole punch**, cut holes for **yarn** so the binoculars can be worn around each child's neck.

Lesson 2 Outing and Parental Supplement

Outing: Sight Nature Walk

Skills: fine motor, following directions, gross motor, sensory development, social-emotional development

Pick a safe location that will have a variety of visual stimuli. (You may want to bring the walking rope from the materials bin for this outing.) Remind the parents and children to bring the binoculars they made earlier in the week. Search for sights from the checklist provided in Lesson 2 Images (booklet of lesson images), or create your own customized list for your location.

Parental Supplement

Books:

- *What Is Sight?* by Molly Aloian (advanced)
- *The Five Senses* by Keith Faulkner
- *Science Experiments with Sight & Sound* by Alex Kuskowski
- *Brown Bear, Brown Bear, What Do You See?* by Bill Martin Jr.
- Any *I Spy* book by Jean Marzollo
- *Five for a Little One* by Chris Raschka
- *Curious George: What Do You See? (A Book of Mirrors)* by H. A. Rey
- *Look! A Book!* by Bob Staake
- *Fun with My 5 Senses* by Sarah A. Williamson
- *Baby Bear Sees Blue* by Ashley Wolff

Activities:

- Compare the color of everyone's eyes in the family.
- Our eyes help us recognize familiar faces. Look through pictures of family and friends.
- Discuss how we can see only when there is light. Have fun playing with flashlights.
- Add colored cellophane to your child's binoculars to explore seeing with colors.
- Try an activity from the book *Science Experiments with Sight & Sound* by Alex Kuskowski.
- Try an activity from the book *Fun with My 5 Senses* by Sarah A. Williamson.

Discussion:

- Discuss what it means to be blind and/or why people wear glasses.
- Discuss colors and how they can't be felt, smelled, or heard. You have to see them.

Resources Used by Authors:

- www.clker.com

Unit 1: Exploring Our Senses
Lesson 3: Sense of Hearing

Lesson Objective: Help the children understand what they hear and what those sounds mean.

Lesson 3 Skill Objectives:

- Attention span
- Emotional awareness
- Fine motor
- Following directions
- Gross motor
- Listening
- Music appreciation
- Patience
- Receptive learning
- Responsibility
- Rhyming
- Sensory development
- Social-emotional development
- Taking turns
- Visual tracking

Preparation

Lesson Materials:

- Blindfolds
- List of sounds that can be created in the classroom (doorbell, telephone, microwave, running faucet, etc.)
- Recording of other sounds children can recognize (dog barking, siren, car engine starting, etc.)

Hands-on Activity Materials:

- Portable timer, cell phone, or metronome

Lesson 3 Outline

1. Welcome music/gather to carpets

2. Welcome song: "The More We Get Together"

3. Attention grabber: Hocus Pocus, Everybody Focus!
   Skills: following directions, visual tracking

4. Calendar time
   Skills: patience, taking turns

5. Story time: *The Ear Book* by Al Perkins
   Skills: attention span, listening, sensory development

6. Transition activity: Preschool Musical Chairs
   Skills: following directions, gross motor, listening, musical appreciation

7. Lesson: What Do You Hear?
   Skills: curiosity, sensory development

8. Hands-on activity: Can You Find It?
   Skills: responsibility, sensory development, taking turns

9. Theme song

10. Children dismissed for free play

Lesson 3 Details

Teacher Tip: Keep It Simple

As you are new to the structure (and possible teaching in general), have realistic expectations of yourself and the children. Take time to let the children get their wiggles out and discuss tangent ideas. There is a lot of natural energy in a preschool classroom! Enjoy it with them and gently guide them back to the lesson's activities. Throughout the year, you will see their attention spans increase. We kept our lesson plans simple on purpose. While we love to see parents' unique approaches and additions to lessons, don't feel like you need to make each lesson like a spectacular themed birthday party, complete with decorations, home-baked treats, and hours of preparation. Keep it simple, and enjoy the growing process together.

Transition Activity: Preschool Musical Chairs

Skills: following directions, gross motor, listening, musical appreciation

Turn on some music. (You can use the music from the LMG SUGGESTED SONG LIST.) Have the children circle around chairs or their mats. Remind them that they must listen for the music to turn off so they can know when to sit quickly back in a seat. (The point is listening, not competition, so make sure there are enough chairs for everyone.) Play several rounds.

Lesson: What Do You Hear?

Skills: curiosity, sensory development

1. Blindfold the children, either one at a time or all together, depending on the size and cooperation level of your group.

2. Explain how their ability to hear with their ears can also help them identify different things or people even when they can't see.

3. Create or play several sounds, like a doorbell or telephone ringing, a microwave dinging, a faucet running, or a dog barking. Have them identify the sounds.

4. Discuss what different noises can tell us and how we know to react to the things we hear.
    a. When we hear a knock at the door, what should we do? (Answer the door because it means someone wants to come in.)
    b. When we hear a fire engine siren, what should we do? (Quickly move out of the way because the firefighters are hurrying to help someone.)

Hands-on Activity: Can You Find It?

Skills: responsibility, sensory development, taking turns

Hide the **portable timer**, **cell phone**, or **metronome** while the children cover their eyes. Have them listen for the sound and try to find the object. If the children are still interested after a few rounds, have them take turns hiding it for each other. If the children lose interest, change the game to hide and seek: let one child hide, then make a sound to help the others find him.

Lesson 3 Outing and Parental Supplement

Outing: Sound Scavenger Hunt

Skills: fine motor, following directions, gross motor, sensory development, social-emotional development

Go on a sound scavenger hunt. (Be sure to choose a different location from last week's outing so the children don't confuse sight and sound.) For a trip to the mall, use the checklist in Lesson 3 Images (booklet of lesson images), or create your own list customized to your location.

Parental Supplement

Books:

- *Tap Tap Boom Boom* by Elizabeth Bluemle
- *Clang! Clang! Beep! Beep!* by Robert Burleigh
- *The Five Senses* by Keith Faulkner
- *Science Experiments with Sight & Sound* by Alex Kuskowski
- *Can You Hear It?* By William Lach
- *Polar Bear, Polar Bear, What Do You Hear?* by Bill Martin Jr. (Note to teacher: If available at your local library, pick the version of this book with the sound panel that makes different animal noises. Children will enjoy pressing the buttons, and it will reinforce the concept of things that make noise.)
- *Too Much Noise* by Ann McGovern
- *The Ear Book* by Al Perkins
- *Five for a Little One* by Chris Raschka
- *Mr. Brown Can Moo, Can You?* by Dr. Seuss
- *A Giraffe and a Half* by Shel Silverstein (a good one to learn and discuss rhyming)
- *Fun with My 5 Senses* by Sarah A. Williamson

Activities:

- Go outside at night and listen. Talk to your child about the things he hears at night and how they are different than what we hear during the day.
- Show your child several different objects (like pennies, cotton balls, or bouncy balls), and have him close his eyes. Place one of these objects into a box and hide the rest of the items. Have your child shake the container, and see if he can guess which item is in the box based on how it sounds.
- Read some age-appropriate poems with your child and discuss how rhyming means words have the same sounds. (Dr. Seuss books are perfect for this!) Practice picking out words that rhyme.

- Listen to all different types of music together. Talk about how different things we hear can affect the way we feel. Dance to different types of music. Move differently depending on how the music sounds.
- Play musical chairs as a family.
- Try an activity from the book *Fun with My 5 Senses* by Sarah A. Williamson.

Discussion:
- Throughout the week, frequently draw your child's attention to things that he can hear. Practice identifying things by their sounds.
- Discuss the difference between loud noises and soft noises. Discuss appropriate places for both.
- Talk about how different sounds can make us feel. Some sounds make us feel happy (like a loved one's voice). Some sounds make us feel peaceful or calm (like quiet music). Some sounds make us feel frightened (like loud fire alarms).
- Talk about how we can recognize familiar people by hearing their voices. At the dinner table, have your child close his eyes, and have someone in the family talk. Have your child guess who is talking based on the sound of the speaker's voice.

Resources Used by Authors:
- www.clker.com

Unit 1: Exploring Our Senses
Lesson 4: Sense of Smell

Lesson Objective: Learn how some common items smell while exploring our own senses of smell.

Lesson 4 Skill Objectives:

- Creativity
- Critical thinking
- Curiosity
- Fine motor
- Following directions
- Imaginative play

- Listening
- Patience
- Responsibility
- Sensory development
- Social-emotional development
- Taking turns

Preparation

Lesson Materials:

- Foods with a scent
- Perfume or air freshener
- Scratch 'n sniff stickers

- Sock puppet
- Lesson 4 Images, already cut out
- Craft sticks (optional)

Hands-on Activity Materials:

- Scented paint (several different Kool-Aid flavors, cornstarch, water)
- Cupcake trays

- Paper
- Brushes or cotton swabs (if painting)

Parent Responsibility:

- Send child with a shirt that can get paint on it

Lesson 4 Outline

1. Welcome music/gather to carpets

2. Welcome song: "The More We Get Together"

3. Attention grabber: Hands on Top, That Means Stop!
   Skills: following directions, listening

4. Calendar time
   Skills: patience, taking turns

5. Story time: *Digger and Daisy Go on a Picnic* by Judy Young
   Skill: attention span

6. Transition activity: Simon Says

7. Lesson: Sense of Smell
   Skills: imaginative play, responsibility, sensory development

8. Hands-on activity: Scented Paints
   Skills: curiosity, creativity, fine motor, sensory development

9. Theme song

10. Children dismissed for free play

Lesson 4 Details

Teacher Tip: Create Hands-on Lessons

Throughout the year, you will find that allowing children to use their hands during a lesson increases their attention spans and improves their ability to learn. This particular lesson utilizes a hand puppet and small cutouts for each child to hold. Make sure your sock puppet interacts directly with each child's cutout, giving the children both tactile and visual stimulation to internalize and interact with. As you teach in coming weeks and months, continue to watch for ways to involve the children's sensory learning skills, thus allowing for increased participation and an improved learning experience.

Transition Activity: Simon Says

Have children stand and copy your movements after you say, "Simon says." For an easier version of the game, always say, "Simon says." For more advanced play, say, "Simon says" only sometimes. Pick movements that require some exertion and get them exercising, like marching, jumping, touching toes (try opposite arm/foot), and arm circles.

Lesson: Sense of Smell

Skills: imaginative play, responsibility, sensory development

1. Provide a variety of items for the children to smell, like food, perfumes, or scratch 'n sniff stickers.

2. Ask the following questions:
    a. "What are some things that smell good?" (Mention food, flowers, and candles.)
    b. "What are some things that smell stinky?" (Mention feet, skunks, and garbage.)
    c. Allow the children to list as many things as they would like. You will probably have to prompt them. As you list the ones above, hand the corresponding cutouts to the children. (The cutouts can be mounted on craft sticks for easier handling.)

3. Tell the following short story about smells. Use the sock puppet (Schnoz) to act out the story. As each child's item is mentioned, have her hold it up and say the accompanying italicized phrase listed in the story. Feel free to ask critical thinking questions during the story.

4. "There once was a three-year-old named Shnoz, who went on an adventure! He had traveled for a long time to get to Uncle Pete's Aroma-Farm. He got out of the car, and the

first thing he saw were some **flowers**! *("Sniff', sniff," ah…)* They were such beautiful **flowers** *("sniff, sniff," ah…)* with lots of colors and wonderful scents. But then he saw something hiding in the flowers. He got closer to look and saw that it was a **skunk**! *(Pee-yew!)* Luckily, the **skunk** *(pee-yew!)* was sleeping, so Shnoz snuck away quietly and didn't have to smell the **skunk's** *(pee-yew!)* stinky spray. Shnoz decided to go into the farmhouse to relax. As he was walking toward the house, he smelled something yucky! He looked around. What could it be? Then he noticed the **garbage cans**. *(Yuck!)* They were overflowing with **garbage** *(yuck!)* and smelled really gross. So he hurried into the house. He sat on the couch and took off his shoes to relax. Uncle Pete came in and said, "What is that smell?" It was Shnoz's **feet**. *(Stinky!)* Shnoz didn't know that his **feet** *(stinky!)* could be so smelly! Uncle Pete decided to light a **candle**. *(Mmm!)* The room started to smell pleasant again because the **candle** *(mmm!)* was beautifully scented. Shnoz realized he was very hungry, so he went in the kitchen where he could smell **dinner cooking**. *(Yum, yum!)* After he ate all of his delicious **food** *(yum, yum!)*, he was tired. So he got ready for bed, went to sleep, and dreamed about all of his scented adventures!"

Hands-on Activity: Scented Paints

Skills: curiosity, creativity, fine motor, sensory development

To make homemade **scented paint**, mix one packet of **Kool-Aid** with 2 tablespoons of **cornstarch** and ½ cup of **water**. (Continue to add cornstarch until you reach desired consistency.) Use different Kool-Aid flavors to create different colors and scents. Divide scented paint into **cupcake trays** or small containers. You can also mix Kool-Aid packets into store-bought washable paints.

Invite the students to paint freely on **paper** using **brushes** or **cotton swabs**. Encourage children's creativity as you help them smell the paint and discuss which flavors or scents they are using.

Note to teacher: The paint may stain, so have bibs, drapes, or adult-sized t-shirts ready for covering clothes. You can also tell parents to send shirts that can get paint on them.

Lesson 4 Outing and Parental Supplement

Outing: Candle Store

Skills: curiosity, sensory development, social-emotional development

Visit a candle store (or bath and body store) and explore the many scents. Try guiding the children in guessing some of the scents. Talk about which ones they do and do not like.

Parental Supplement

Books:

- *The Five Senses* by Keith Faulkner
- *I Smell…* by Patrick George
- *The Story of Ferdinand* by Munro Leaf
- *A Whiff and a Sniff* by Jane Belk Moncure
- *The Nose Book* by Al Perkins (version illustrated by Joe Mathieu)
- *Five for a Little One* by Chris Raschka
- *Fun with My 5 Senses* by Sarah A. Williamson
- *Digger and Daisy Go on a Picnic* by Judy Young

Activities:

- When cooking a meal, have your child guess what is being made, just from the smell.
- Help your child explore the smells of various spices and seasonings.
- Make any craft together with scratch 'n sniff stickers or scented paint.
- Guess the scent! Put something strong smelling (like freshly baked cookies, an orange, flowers, or a familiar perfume) in a canister. Place holes in the top, small enough so your child can't see inside, but large enough so she can smell the object. Have her guess.
- Have your child smell scented candles at a store. Have her guess the scents, or talk about which ones she likes and doesn't like.
- Visit a flower garden.
- Visit a bakery. Talk about how smells and tastes relate.
- Make your own play dough. Add spices or essential oils to scent it.
- Try an activity from the book *Fun with My 5 Senses* by Sarah A. Williamson.

Discussion:

- Talk about your nose and how we sniff in order to smell. Practice sniffing.
- Point out that our noses are also used for breathing.
- Discuss the importance of bathing and showering to keep ourselves smelling clean.
- Talk about your favorite and least favorite smells.

- Discuss how smells can warn us. Discuss smoke and fires, how we respond to those smells, and other safety issues.

Resources Used by Authors:
- www.clker.com

Unit 1: Exploring Our Senses
Lesson 5: Sense of Taste

Lesson Objective: Help the children understand and explore their sense of taste, what tastes good to them, and what kinds of different tastes they can experience.

Lesson 5 Skill Objectives:

- Attention span
- Curiosity
- Critical thinking
- Curiosity
- Following directions
- Gross motor
- Imaginative play
- Listening
- Patience
- Sensory development
- Social-emotional development
- Taking turns

Preparation

Lesson Materials:

- Lesson 5 Images

Hands-on Activity Materials:

- Blindfolds
- Graham crackers
- Apples (red and green)
- Cheese slices
- Milk chocolate
- Lemon
- Tortilla or potato chips
- 80% dark chocolate
- Any other foods you prefer to use

Lesson 5 Outline

5. Welcome music/gather to carpets

6. Welcome song: "The More We Get Together"

7. Attention grabber: Do What I'm Doing!
   Skill: following directions

8. Calendar time
   Skills: patience, taking turns

9. Story time: *The Little Mouse, the Red Ripe Strawberry, and the Big Hungry Bear* by Don Wood
   Skills: attention span, listening

10. Transition activity: Peanut Butter and Jelly
    Skills: imaginative play, gross motor

11. Lesson: Sense of Taste
    Skills: curiosity, sensory development, taking turns

12. Hands-on activity: Taste Testing
    Skills: critical thinking, sensory development

13. Theme song

14. Children dismissed for free play

Lesson 5 Details

Teacher Training Tip: Encourage Opinions

One of your teaching roles includes helping children develop their own opinions, sense of individuality, and confidence. Throughout the year, encourage them to answer questions honestly and discuss their own unique opinions. In this lesson, for example, do not focus on promoting healthy food choices (that will come in Lesson 14). Instead, praise the children for their unique opinions and validate their individual likes and dislikes. For example, if one child says he hates broccoli, acknowledge that as an appropriate opinion, and ask the other children how they feel. They can then have confidence as they respond, as there are no right or wrong answers to questions in this lesson.

Transition Activity: Peanut Butter and Jelly

Skills: imaginative play, gross motor

With everyone standing, recite or sing the following song while doing the italicized actions. Feel free to make comments as you go about how the peanut butter and jelly feel, taste, and look to gear the children's minds towards sensory learning. Introduce the lesson by talking about how good the sandwich tastes. Does this make them hungry for yummy foods that taste good?

> Peanut butter, peanut butter *(reach arms high to the right)*
> And jelly *(reach arms down to the left)*
> Peanut butter, peanut butter *(reach arms high to the right)*
> And jelly *(reach arms down to the left)*
>
> First you get the peanuts, and you pick 'em, you pick 'em,
> You pick 'em, pick 'em, pick 'em *(pretend to pick peanuts)*.
> And you smash 'em, you smash 'em,
> You smash 'em, smash 'em, smash 'em *(pretend to smash between your hands)*.
> And you spread 'em, you spread 'em,
> You spread 'em, spread 'em, spread 'em *(pretend to spread on bread)*.
>
> Next you get the berries, and you pick 'em, you pick 'em,
> You pick 'em, pick 'em, pick 'em *(pretend to pick berries)*.
> And you smash 'em, you smash 'em,
> You smash 'em, smash 'em, smash 'em *(pretend to smash)*.
> And you spread 'em, you spread 'em,
> You spread 'em, spread 'em, spread 'em *(pretend to spread on bread)*.

Then you take the sandwich, and you bite it, you bite it,
You bite it, bite it, bite it *(pretend to bite sandwich).*
And you chew it, you chew it,
You chew it, chew it, chew it *(pretend to chew sandwich).*
And you swallow it, you swallow it,
You swallow it, swallow it, swallow it *(pretend to swallow with difficulty because it is so sticky).*

MMMmmmmmmmm! MMMmmmmmmmm!

Lesson: Sense of Taste

Skills: curiosity, sensory development, taking turns

1. Today we are learning about things that we taste. Ask the children if they know what part of their body they use to taste things.

2. Talk to them about their tongue. Have them all stick out their tongues. Have them touch their tongues with their fingers and feel the bumps on their tongues. Explain that those **taste buds* help them taste!

3. Discuss the difference in things that taste good and things that taste bad. Ask them the following questions, and allow each child to answer:
    a. What is your favorite thing to eat for breakfast?
    b. What is your favorite food that your mom or dad makes for dinner?
    c. Do you have a favorite treat?
    d. What food do you not like to eat?

4. Show them the pictures of the following food items (found in Lesson 5 Images), and ask them if each thing tastes good or bad to them. You can also talk about what textures each food has.
    a. Apples
    b. Broccoli
    c. Chicken and potatoes
    d. Popcorn
    e. Green salad
    f. Pancakes or waffles
    g. Pizza
    h. Chocolate chip cookies
    i. Dirt (just to make sure they are paying attention!)

Hands-on Activity: Taste Testing

Skills: critical thinking, sensory development

1. Have children gather around a table. Explain that sometimes we can learn what something is by the way it tastes.

2. For the first few foods, **blindfold** the children. Instruct them that they will open their mouths and then tell you what they are eating based on how it tastes. Use the following (or any other) foods that will be familiar to them and easy to identify:
    a. **Graham crackers**
    b. **Apples** (red and green)
    c. **Cheese**

3. As they identify the foods, explain that their tongues told them what they were tasting.

4. Remove the blindfolds and continue talking and eating!

5. Explain that there are four different types of tastes, and then give them an example of each kind to try:
    a. Sweet: Hand out small pieces of **milk chocolate**, chocolate chips, or cookies
    b. Sour: Slice up a **lemon** and let each child lick a wedge
    c. Salty: Give each child a **tortilla or potato chip**
    d. Bitter: Hand out **80% dark chocolate** pieces
    e. Optional: discuss spicy foods

6. Discussion items:
    a. Which of the four types of tastes was your favorite? Isn't it neat how much our tongues can tell us?
    b. What was the difference in the taste of the red and green apples?
    c. Can you think of any other foods that are sweet, sour, salty, or bitter?

Lesson 5 Outing and Parental Supplement

Outing: Taste Testers

Skills: curiosity, gross motor, sensory development, social-emotional development

Visit a local candy factory, bakery, or grocery store where you can watch some kind of food being made. (Optimally, choose a place that gives out samples for you to taste test when the food is done.) Draw the children's attention to the different ingredients that make the finished product taste a certain way. (Ex: "Look, they are putting all of that sugar in now! That is what will make the candy taste extra sweet when it's done!")

Parental Supplement

Books:

- *What Is Taste?* by Jennifer Boothroyd
- *D.W., the Picky Eater* by Marc Tolon Brown
- *I Taste, Sing, and Read* by Joann Cleland
- *The Five Senses* by Keith Faulkner
- *I Taste...* by Patrick George
- *Bread and Jam for Frances* by Russell Hoban
- *Five for a Little One* by Chris Raschka
- *Green Eggs and Ham* by Dr. Seuss
- *Fun with My 5 Senses* by Sarah A. Williamson
- *The Little Mouse, the Red Ripe Strawberry, and the Big Hungry Bear* by Don Wood

Activities:

- Encourage your child to help you prepare at least one meal or snack this week. As you work together, encourage your child to taste some of the different ingredients and decide how each of these ingredients taste to them.
- Add some variety by introducing new foods that your child may not be used to. Encourage him to try the new foods, and talk about why he does or does not like the new foods.
- Go to Costco together, and sample several different food items. Have your child decide which samples he enjoyed most.
- Sorting is a great way to prepare your preschooler for math. Provide different types of food and practice sorting the food into piles (Ex: candy pieces go in the sweet pile, while chips go in the salty pile.)
- Try an activity from the book *Fun with My 5 Senses* by Sarah A. Williamson.

Discussion:

- Point out when your child is eating something sweet, sour, salty, or bitter.
- Freely discuss tastes that you like and dislike as well. Explain that things that taste good to one person may not taste good to another, and that it's ok to have different opinions, likes, and dislikes.
- In-home discussions are the most appropriate place for teaching healthy options for food. Explain that we need to keep trying healthy foods even if we don't always like the way they taste.

Resources Used by Authors:
- Church, Ellen Booth. *Terrific Transitions*. (Transition activity taken directly from this book.)
- http://kidshealth.org/kid/htbw/_bfs_TTactivity.html
  http://voices.yahoo.com/terrific-childrens-books-sense-taste-lesson-11969453.html
- www.clker.com

Unit 1: Exploring Our Senses
Lesson 6: Sense of Touch

Lesson Objective: Learn new adjectives while exploring how things feel.

Lesson 2 Skill Objectives:

- Attention span
- Critical thinking
- Creativity
- Expressive language
- Fine motor
- Following directions
- Gross motor
- Patience
- Sensory development
- Social-emotional development
- Taking turns
- Vocabulary

Preparation

Lesson Materials:

- Several objects that feel unique (ex: pompom balls, feathers, beans/bean bag, ice, tape, sandpaper)
- A box or bowl to hide items in
- Paper
- Glue

Hands-on Activity Materials:

- Play dough
- Beans or beads

Lesson 6 Outline

1. Welcome music/gather to carpets

2. Welcome song: "The More We Get Together"

3. Attention grabber: Stand Up! Sit Down.
   Skills: following directions, gross motor

4. Calendar time
   Skills: patience, taking turns

5. Story time: Choose one or two of your favorite "touch and feel" books
   Skill: attention span

6. Transition activity: I Spy
   Skills: following directions, gross motor, vocabulary

7. Lesson: Sense of Touch
   Skills: critical thinking, expressive language, fine motor, sensory development, patience, vocabulary

8. Hands-on activity: Play dough
   Skills: creativity, expressive development, fine motor, sensory development

9. Theme song

10. Children dismissed for free play

Lesson 6 Details

Teacher Tip: Teach New Words

It is important to expose your preschooler to as many new words as possible. We are aware that children may not fully understand all the terms included in these lessons, but don't let this deter you. An important contributor to early literacy is wide exposure to new vocabulary through reading and talking to your children. Continue to help the children make connections by using new words in context, giving examples, or explaining. Enjoy watching their vocabulary and understanding increase! In this manual, we indicate new words (like *taste bud* in Lesson 5) by italicizing them the first time they are used.

Transition Activity: I Spy

Skills: following directions, gross motor, vocabulary

Pick an item from around the room and explain what it feels like. (Examples: the table is smooth, the wall is bumpy, the stuffed animal is furry, or the fridge feels cold.) Use new adjectives! You may need to give other clues about size, color, or purpose. Have the children guess and then run to that object. Repeat until everyone has had a turn.

Lesson: Sense of Touch

Skills: critical thinking, expressive language, fine motor, sensory development, patience, vocabulary

1. Review the book from story time. What is touch? Our skin can feel things!

2. Bring out the household objects that feel unique (ex: pompom balls, feathers, beans, ice, tape, or sandpaper). If possible, have enough of each item that each child can hold her own.

3. Pass out one type of item at a time so children can focus on the different textures. Give the entire group time to explore the item. Encourage them to touch the items to their cheeks, arms, and legs. Have them describe what textures they feel (fuzzy, soft, sticky, bumpy, etc.).

4. Repeat the exploration and explanation for each item. Teach them new adjectives, and encourage their use of language in their attempts to describe the objects. Try to use a new adjective for each object.

5. Place one of the items in a box and have a child reach inside without looking. See if she can use her new vocabulary to describe what it feels like and guess the item. Have each child take a turn.

6. Make a texture collage by gluing these items to paper. Be sure to supervise the gluing!

Hands-on Activity: Play dough

Skills: creativity, expressive development, fine motor, sensory development

Allow the children to play freely with **play dough**. Hide items like **beads**, **beans**, or small toys in the play dough. Have them feel for the hard items in the soft play dough. As they play and sculpt, ask what they are feeling with their sense of touch.

Lesson 6 Outing and Parental Supplement

Outing: Spa Day

Skills: sensory development, social-emotional development

Introduce the children to different textures as you treat them to manicures, pedicures, massages, or facials at home or at a salon. Discuss temperatures, textures, and pressures as you take care of their hands, feet, and skin. Remember that manicures don't have to include nail polish! Also, while manicures and pedicures may be more exciting to girls, boys can still enjoy massages.

Parental Supplement

Books:

- Any "touch and Feel" book by any author
- *What Is Touch?* by Jennifer Boothroyd
- *I Face the Wind* by Vicki Cobb (advanced)
- *The Five Senses* by Keith Faulkner
- *Hands Can* by Cheryl Willis Hudson
- *Elmo Can . . . Taste! Touch! Smell! See! Hear!* by Michaela Muntean
- *Five for a Little One* by Chris Raschka
- *Press Here* by Herve Tullet
- *Fun with My 5 Senses* by Sarah A. Williamson

Activities:

- Do a texture tracing activity together. Placing textured items under paper, and color the paper with crayon on top to see and feel the textures.
- Talk about how the sense of touch is not limited to just our hands. Draw shapes or letters on your child's back with your finger. See if he can guess what you drew!
- Have a tickle fight. Explain that his feet and other parts of his body can feel too.
- Repeat the play dough activity at home with new objects.
- Weather permitting, walk outside together in your bare feet. Find a variety of surfaces and talk about how each feels.
- Go to a fabric store. (Make sure hands are clean!) Touch the different fabrics and discuss how they feel. Which is his favorite?
- Finger paint.
- Try an activity from the book *Fun with My 5 Senses* by Sarah A. Williamson.

Discussion:

- Look for opportunities throughout the week to point out what your child is feeling with his sense of touch. Discuss this as it relates to his toys, clothes, food, and other textures.

- Discuss what happens when we touch something that is very hot or cold. Explain any safety issues that your child may need to learn related to the sense of touch. (A more extensive lesson on safety will be taught in Lesson 15.)

Unit 2: Things That Are Alive
Lesson 7: Farm Animals

Lesson Objective: Learn more about several different farm animals in a fun and interactive environment.

Lesson 7 Skill Objectives:

- Attention span
- Creativity
- Critical thinking
- Curiosity
- Decision making
- Fine motor
- Following directions
- Gross motor

- Imaginative play
- Listening
- Music appreciation
- Patience
- Sensory development
- Social-emotional development
- Taking turns
- Vocabulary

Preparation

Transition Activity Materials:

- Lesson 7 Images (pages 1–2)
- LMG SUGGESTED SONG LIST

Lesson Materials:

- Blankets
- Chairs
- Baby gate (optional)
- Bell (for cows)
- Rope (for horses)
- Sunflower seeds, chocolate covered or regular (for chickens)
- Large pretzel sticks (for dogs)
- Bowl with milk (for cats)
- Brown blanket or tarp (for pigs)
  Note: gather props only for the 2–3 animals you choose to focus on

Hands-on Activity Materials:

- Cutouts of farm animal paper bag puppets (from internet)
- Coloring materials
- Glue sticks
- Brown paper bags

Lesson 7 Outline

11. Welcome music/gather to carpets

12. Welcome song: "The More We Get Together"

13. Attention grabber: Stand Up! Sit Down.
    Skills: following directions, gross motor

14. Calendar time
    Skills: patience, taking turns

15. Story time: *Cock-a-Doodle-Doo, Creak, Pop-Pop, Moo* by Jim Ayelsworth
    Skills: attention span, listening

16. Transition activity: "Old McDonald Had a Farm"
    Skills: music appreciation, taking turns

17. Lesson: Animals on the Farm
    Skills: critical thinking, gross motor, vocabulary

18. Hands-on activity: Farm Animal Puppets
    Skills: creativity, decision making, fine motor, imagination

19. Theme song

20. Children dismissed for free play

Lesson 7 Details

Teacher Tip: Avoid the Fact Trap

When teaching Unit 2, keep the focus on the imaginative, activity-based portion of the lesson (pretending to be farm animals, in this case). The facts about how the animals eat, sleep, move, and talk are only intended to supplement the main activity—you should not try to teach all (or even most) of them. Always focus on the children's excitement during the learning process, not on teaching them facts to memorize. Whether you teach them one fact or twenty, as long as they are playing, imagining and having fun, they are learning! Focus on the play, and the learning will happen naturally. You will be amazed at how much they remember later!

Transition Activity: "Old McDonald Had a Farm"

Skills: music appreciation, taking turns

Allow each child to pick a cutout of a different animal from **Lesson 7 Images**. Play "Old McDonald Had a Farm" (#11 on the **LMG SUGGESTED SONG LIST**). As you sing the song, have the children take turns holding up their animal and saying the appropriate animal sound.

Lesson: Animals on the Farm

Skills: critical thinking, gross motor, vocabulary

1. Before the lesson, prepare the following:
    a. Create a barn with **blankets** or **chairs** (much like you'd create a fort).
    b. Create a pasture by enclosing a separate space using chairs or a **baby gate**.
    c. Choose 2–3 animals from the list provided and be ready with the appropriate props so the children can pretend to be those animals. (Continue longer as attention spans permit.)
    d. Before the children arrive, make sure you have read through the fun facts for each animal. Be ready to teach ONE fact for each animal you have chosen. (Optimally, you won't need to refer to your manual during the lesson.)
        i. As the children show interest, throw in other activities or discussions based on the facts and suggestions listed below. Some groups may enjoy walking, talking, acting like, sleeping, and pretending to eat like several of the animals. Some children will only have the attention for one focused activity per animal before you need to move on.
        ii. This approach will allow you to cater to the children's needs and attention spans. Once again, don't feel pressured to get through a list of

facts—the facts are merely intended to supplement the imaginative part of the lesson

2. As the children pretend to be the different animals, use the props provided and have them move from the pasture into the barn where the animals might eat, or go to sleep for the night.
    a. Cow: Use the **cow bell** as the children walk to the barn. Refer to the fun facts below as needed.
    b. Horse: Use a **rope** to lead the "horses" into the barn. They may wish to gallop like horses and say "neigh!" Refer to the other fun facts below as needed.
    c. Chickens: Practice pecking at **sunflower seeds** like chickens do. The children may wish to walk or talk like chickens while looking for their meal or moving to the barn. Refer to the fun facts below as needed.
    d. Dogs: Practice playing fetch with the **large pretzel sticks**. Refer to the fun facts below as needed.
    e. Cats: Find a place where it's ok to make messes and practice lapping up **milk in a bowl** like cats do! Refer to the fun facts below as needed.
    f. Pigs: Use your **blanket or tarp** to pretend you are rolling in the mud to stay cool like pigs do. Refer to fun facts below as needed.

FUN FACTS (to supplement the activities above)
1. Fun facts: cows
    a. Eat: Cows eat grass.
    b. Sleep: They sleep standing up in a barn or in a field. Cows only sleep four hours a day.
    c. Move: They walk on all four legs. Often times they travel in *herds* led by a dominant male. (Optional: Have the children take turns pretending to be the dominant male and lead the rest of the children as they crawl around on the floor pretending to be cows.)
    d. Talk: Cows say, "MOOOOO."
    e. Fun fact: Cows often wear bells around their necks so they are easy for farmers to find!

2. Fun facts: horses
    a. Eat: They eat hay, *grains*, and grass.
    b. Sleep: They sleep in a barn or in a field, standing up or lying down. They only sleep 3 hours a day and for 15 minutes at a time.
    c. Move: They walk, trot, or gallop. (Optional: Practice doing each one together.)
    d. Talk: Horses say, "Neigh."
    e. Fun fact: Horses are one of the few animals that humans ride on. (Optional: Take turns giving horse rides.

3. Fun facts: chickens
    a. Eat: They eat seeds and bugs.
    b. Sleep: Chickens sleep in chicken coops.
    c. Move: They walk on two legs or fly short distances. (Optional: Demonstrate the funny walk of a chicken. Have the children mimic you.)
    d. Talk: Chickens say, "Bawk bawk."
    e. Fun fact: Chicken babies come from eggs. After a chicken lays the eggs, she sits on them until the eggs *hatch*. (Optional: Discuss, "Chickens also lay eggs for us to eat! Do you like to eat scrambled eggs? Those are made by chickens!")

4. Fun facts: dogs
    a. Eat: Dogs eat dog food and some people food.
    b. Sleep: They sleep lying down, curled up with their head in their paws. They like to sleep in a doghouse, outside, or in your bed! (Optional: Demonstrate how dogs curl up to sleep.)
    c. Move: They walk on all four legs. Dogs can also be taught fun tricks, like standing up on two legs or running to fetch something.
    d. Talk: Dogs can say, "Woof woof," "Bow wow," or make howling noises. (Optional: Practice making all the noises together to sound like a *pack* of dogs!)
    e. Fun fact: Dogs have an incredible sense of smell. Dogs are often used to find people who are lost because dogs can smell them from far away!

5. Fun facts: cats
    a. Eat: Cats eat cat food and milk.
    b. Sleep: They sleep curled up in warm places and on your bed! (Optional: Ask the children if any of them have a cat. Where do their cats sleep?)
    c. Move: They walk on all four legs.
    d. Talk: Cats say, "Meow."
    e. Fun fact: Cats are very good at landing on their feet! Cats are also very clean. They clean themselves, and their babies, by licking.

6. Fun facts: pigs
    a. Eat: Pigs eat leftovers! They love to eat leftover dinner, even things that people don't eat, like watermelon rinds. Pigs are very noisy and messy eaters.
    b. Sleep: They sleep lying down. They don't mind lying in big piles of dirt or mud.
    c. Move: They walk on all four legs.
    d. Talk: Pigs say, "Oink oink" or make snorting noises.
    e. Fun fact: Pigs love to roll in the mud to cool off.

Hands-on Activity: Farm Animal Puppets

Skills: creativity, decision making, fine motor, imagination

Before the lesson, search online for "**farm animal paper bag puppets**." Print and cut out your favorites. Allow the children to **color** their cutouts, and help them **glue** the pieces onto their **paper bags** appropriately to make puppets. If time and attention span allow, have the children put on a puppet show together. Give them some direction (like a basic storyline or a scenario to start them out), and allow them to interact with each other and use their imaginations.

Lesson 7 Outing and Parental Supplement

Outing: Farm

Skills: curiosity, gross motor, sensory development, social-emotional development

Visit a local farm (commercial or private) or petting zoo, depending on what is available in your area. (If there are no farms in your area, find a pet store or a pet owner who will allow the children to come and play with the animals.) Encourage the children to interact with the animals. Encourage them to notice how the animals eat, sleep, move, and talk.

Parental Supplement

Books

- *Farmyard Beat* by Lindsey Craig
- *Click, Clack, Moo: Cows That Type* by Doreen Cronin
- *Dooby Dooby Moo* by Doreen Cronin
- *I Spy on the Farm* by Edward Gibbs
- *Real-size Farm Animals* by Marie Greenwood
- *Everyone Sleeps* by Marcellus Hall
- *Big Chickens Fly the Coop* by Leslie Helakoski
- *Old MacDonald Had a Farm* by Anne Kennedy
- *Little Blue Truck* by Alice Schertle

Activities

- Repeat the activity from the lesson and make your living room or playroom into a barn. Pretend to be different animals and see if your child can remember how they eat, sleep, move, and talk.
- If you have toy farm animals or stuffed animals at home, play with those. Allow your child to direct the play, and follow his lead.
- If you have access to someone with horses, set up a time that you can take your child to ride on a horse. If you do not, find anyone with domestic animals that would allow you to come play with, pet, or observe the animals.
- Make simple finger puppets together, and sing the song "Five Little Ducks."
- Sing "Old MacDonald had a Farm" together. Let your child choose the animals.
- Look through books or encyclopedias to learning about some of the farm animals not covered in this lesson or review ones that your child is excited about from the lesson.

Discussion

- Have your child ask several family members or friends what their favorite farm animals are and why. Ask your child to tell you what his favorite is, and ask if he can tell you why. While he may not be able to articulate why yet, it will help him to start understanding how to think critically as you ask him these questions and help him explore the reasons for his own interests, likes, and dislikes. It also helps him develop a sense of individuality and strengthens his self-esteem as he learns his opinions are important and valued.

- Has your child ever met farm animals before this week's lesson and outing? What are some memories he has?
- Why do farmers keep these animals on the farm? Does your child remember (from the lesson) some of the things farm animals give us or do for us?

Resources Used by Authors
- www.clker.com
- www.eol.org

Unit 2: Things That Are Alive
Lesson 8: Wild Animals

Lesson Objective: Learn more about several different wild animals in a fun and interactive environment.

Lesson 8 Skill Objectives:
- Attention span
- Curiosity
- Decision making
- Following directions
- Gross motor
- Imaginative play
- Initiative
- Patience
- Respect
- Self-esteem
- Sensory development
- Social-emotional development
- Taking turns
- Vocabulary

Preparation

Transition Activity Materials:
- LMG SUGGESTED SONG LIST

Lesson Materials:
- Bag filled with hot dogs
- Bag filled with twigs
- Bag filled with lettuce
- Bag filled with bananas
- Bag filled with grass
- One image of each of the following animals, printed from the internet and hung on a string (to be worn around children's necks): lion, elephant, giraffe, monkey, zebra, and kangaroo

Hands-on Activity Materials:
- None

Lesson 8 Outline

1. Welcome music/gather to carpets

2. Welcome song: "The More We Get Together"

3. Attention grabber: One, Two, Three, Now Follow Me!
   Skill: following directions

4. Calendar time
   Skills: patience, taking turns

5. Story time: *Way Far Away on a Wild Safari* by Jan Peck
   Skill: attention span

6. Transition activity: "The Animal Hokey Pokey"
   Skills: gross motor, imaginative play

7. Lesson: Wild Animals
   Skills: gross motor, imaginative play, initiative, respect, self-esteem, vocabulary

8. Hands-on activity: Safari Races
   Skills: gross motor, imaginative play

9. Theme song

10. Children dismissed for free play

Lesson 8 Details

Teacher Tip: Move

Remember that early childhood learning depends on movement. Throughout this lesson, focus on how you can keep the children engaged through movement! Don't be discouraged if the movement seems to distract from the lesson at times. Instead, participate with them; allow them to enjoy moving, running, and playing; and watch for opportunities to regain participation and attention. (Starting a new activity is a great time to refocus the lesson.)

Remember to avoid the fact trap of merely reciting too many facts in this lesson. Read the Teach Tip in Lesson 7 for more details.

Transition Activity: "The Animal Hokey Pokey"

Skills: gross motor, imaginative play

Dance to the "The Animal Hokey Pokey" (#12 on the **LMG SUGGESTED SONG LIST**).

Lesson: Wild Animals

Skills: gross motor, imaginative play, initiative, respect, self-esteem, vocabulary

1. Before the lesson, review the fun facts for each animal. Be ready to teach one or two facts for each animal. (Optimally, you won't need to refer to your manual during the lesson.)

2. Tell the children that today you will go on a wild animal safari and try to spot different animals! Pretend to get into a Jeep, and use the walking rope to keep the children together as you go on a wild safari adventure, either inside or outside.

3. Give each child a **paper bag** filled with one type of animal food: **hot dogs** (for lions), **twigs** (for elephants), **lettuce** (for giraffes), **bananas** (for chimpanzees), and **grass** (for zebras and kangaroos).

4. Once you are on your safari, have the children take turns choosing an **animal picture** and hiding. Once that child is hidden, have the rest of the group try to find her.

5. Once the animal is found, decide what that animal wants to eat. Whoever has the correct food for that animal in their bag can pretend to feed the animal. (Safety note: emphasize that only trained professionals can feed wild animals.)

6. Use any of the facts or optional activities below to supplement your safari as the children's attention spans allow. Have the child pretending to be each wild animal show you how that animal eats, sleeps, moves or talks if the children are interested. Quickly move on to the next child's turn when the group becomes distracted.

FUN FACTS (to supplement the activities above)
1. Fun facts: elephants
    a. Eat: They eat grass, leaves, and twigs. They spend most of their day eating.
    b. Live/sleep: They live in jungles and grasslands. They make "nest" areas in the ground and sleep there.
    c. Move: They walk on four legs. Because they are so big, they move slowly. They travel in big groups together. Elephants also like to swim.
    d. Talk: They make a trumpeting sound. (Optional: Have the children use their arms as pretend trunks and make an elephant sound.)
    e. Fun fact: Elephants use their trunks to grab things, breathe, smell, touch, spray water, and make trumpeting sounds.

2. Fun facts: lions
    a. Eat: They are *carnivores*, which means they only eat meat.
    b. Live/sleep: Lions live in the African desert and grasslands. They sleep on the ground. Lions rest almost all day—20 hours! (Optional: Show the children where Africa is on a map or globe.)
    c. Move: They walk on four legs. They can run quickly when they are hunting. They can also pounce. (Optional: Have the children pretend to pounce.)
    d. Talk: Lions roar! (Optional: Have the children roar.)
    e. Fun fact: Girl lions do most of the hunting, and they hunt at night. Boy lions grow large manes of hair around their head.

3. Fun facts: giraffes
    a. Eat: They are *herbivores*, which means they only eat plant foods. They like leaves because they can reach the tops of the trees with their long necks. (Optional: Have the children pretend to reach and eat leaves in the trees.)
    b. Live/sleep: They live in the African grasslands.
    c. Move: They walk and run on four legs. They can run at moderate speeds of 35 mph (that's as fast as a car goes!) in a teeter-totter motion.
    d. Talk: They don't make a sound.
    e. Fun fact: Giraffes are the tallest animals! They are six feet tall when they are born—that's about as tall as some of your dads!

4. Fun facts: chimpanzees
    a. Eat: They are *omnivores*, which means they eat plants (fruit and leaves) and meat (insects). They like to eat when they are up in the trees.
    b. Live/sleep: They live in the forest and sleep in the trees.

    c. Move: They can walk on all four legs, stand up and walk, and swing in the trees.
    d. Talk: Chimps are noisy! They hoot, yell, and grunt. (Optional: Make monkey sounds together.)
    e. Fun fact: A baby chimpanzee holds onto his mommy's tummy while she walks around.

5. Fun facts: zebras
    a. Eat: They live in the grasslands and eat grass.
    b. Live/sleep: They sleep standing up.
    c. Move: They run like horses and travel in herds.
    d. Talk: They make sounds like horses, but slightly higher-pitched. (Optional: Make zebra sounds.)
    e. Fun fact: Every zebra has a unique pattern of black and white stripes. (Optional: Talk about how we are all unique, just like zebras! Ask the children, "What are the things about each of us that are also unique?")

6. Fun facts: kangaroos
    a. Eat: They mainly eat grass.
    b. Live/sleep: They live in Australia. They sleep during the day while lying on their sides.
    c. Move: They hop using their big back feet. They are fast! (Optional: Hop around like a kangaroo.)
    d. Talk: They don't make many sounds with their voices, but they do stomp their feet to communicate and warn each other of danger. (Optional: Stomp your feet like a kangaroo.)
    e. Fun fact: A dad kangaroo is called a "boomer," a mom kangaroo is called a "flyer," and a baby kangaroo is called a "joey." A joey is carried in its mother's pouch on her tummy.

Hands-on Activity: Safari Races

Skills: gross motor, imaginative play

Have the children choose together an animal from the lesson or another animal of their choice. Decide together how that animal moves, and let the children race each other while moving like that animal. Repeat using different animals.

Lesson 8 Outing and Parental Supplement

Outing: The Zoo

Skills: curiosity, gross motor, sensory development, social-emotional development

Plan a trip to the zoo to see the wild animals that were covered in this lesson and many more.

Parental Supplement

Books

- *Amazing Animal Facts: A Visual Guide to the World's Most Incredible Creatures* by Jacqui Bailey
- *Gumption!* by Elise Broach
- *If I Were a Jungle Animal* by Amanda Ellery
- *Monkey and Me* by Emily Gravett
- *Everyone Sleeps* by Marcellus Hall
- *Can You See Me?* by Ted Lewin
- *Little Lost Tiger* by Jonathan London
- *Oxford First Book of Animals* by Barbara Taylor

Activities

- Pretend to be a wild animal. See if your child remembers some of the things taught in the lesson.
- Eat animal crackers together and discuss the different wild animals.
- Make a giraffe craft. Have your child paint and decorate a paper towel roll like it's a giraffe neck. When it's dry, attach a cutout in the shape of a giraffe's head.
- Make wild animal paper plate masks together using various paints, construction paper, or markers.
- Cut out craft foam in the shape of a wild animal's footprint. Attach it to the bottom of your child's shoe and go for a walk somewhere where footprints will be left behind. Talk about how animals make different-shaped footprints.

Discussion

- Talk about some wild animals in your local area. Discuss, "What do we know about them? What else should we learn about them?"
- Practice your child's vocabulary while discussing the differences in wild animals. Discuss the differences in their sizes, shapes, abilities, traits, etc. (Ex: "Who has a longer neck, a giraffe or a lion? Who is bigger, an elephant or a monkey?")
- Discuss why safety around wild animals is so important. Teach your children that only trained adults should ever go near an animal in the wild or at the zoo.

Resources Used by Authors
- http://eol.org
- http://kids.nationalgeographic.com/animals/giraffe.html#

Unit 2: Things That Are Alive
Lesson 9: Ocean Animals

Lesson Objective: Learn more about ocean animals in a fun and interactive way.

Lesson 9 Skill Objectives:

- Attention span
- Courage
- Critical thinking
- Curiosity
- Fine motor
- Following directions
- Imaginative play
- Leadership
- Listening
- Patience
- Pre-math
- Sensory development
- Social-emotional development
- Taking turns
- Teamwork
- Vocabulary

Preparation

Transition Activity Materials:

- Bubbles
- Music (optional)

Lesson Materials:

- Another parent to help with the fishing portion of the lesson (optional)
- Sheet
- Pole
- String
- Clothespin
- Cutouts (from internet) of the following animals, mounted on sturdy paper: fish, shark, starfish, whale, crab, jellyfish, blowfish

Hands-on Activity Materials:

- Lesson 9 Images: 10 of each in 2 different sizes and 3 different colors
- OR multicolored baked fish crackers

Lesson 9 Outline

1. Welcome music/gather to carpets

2. Welcome song: "The More We Get Together"

3. Attention grabber: Hands on Top, That Means Stop!
   Skill: following directions, gross motor

4. Calendar time
   Skills: patience, taking turns

5. Story time: *Swimmy* by Leo Lionni (if the children in your group may be frightened by the part where Swimmy's friends get eaten, consider summarizing or rewording)
   Skill: attention span, courage, friendship, leadership, listening, teamwork

6. Transition activity: Bubbles
   Skills: gross motor, sensory development

7. Lesson: Go Fish
   Skills: curiosity, critical thinking, fine motor, gross motor, imaginative play, vocabulary

8. Hands-on activity: Fish Sorting
   Skill: pre-math

9. Theme song

10. Children dismissed for free play

Lesson 9 Details

Teacher Tip: Facilitate Curiosity

As you ask the children questions throughout each lesson and outing, remember your objective. The purpose of this curriculum is not to force or even encourage memorization of facts. It is to spark their curiosity and inspire them to begin the process of thinking critically. As you ask questions, allow their little minds time to process the information and become excited about sharing the things they are learning. Continue to challenge them without forcing them. Set aside the desire to quiz and extract information, but instead become a facilitator of their curiosity and discovery!

Remember to avoid the fact trap of merely reciting too many facts in this lesson. Read the Teacher Tip in Lesson 7 for more details.

Transition Activity: Bubbles

Skills: gross motor, sensory development

Get out some **bubbles** and blow them for the children for no more than 3–5 minutes as a way to get wiggles out! You can play **music** while you're blowing bubbles. Use this activity as a lead-in to the lesson portion. (Ex: "We can also blow bubbles under water. Today we are going to talk about animals that live in the water."

Lesson: Go Fish

Skills: curiosity, critical thinking, fine motor, gross motor, imaginative play, vocabulary

1. Before the lesson prepare the following:
    a. Ask **another parent to help** with the fishing portion of the lesson (optional).
    b. Hang up a **sheet**, preferably blue, on one side of the room, so children can go "fishing" for ocean animals. Hang it high enough so that the children cannot see over the top.
    c. Create a fishing pole from a **pole**, **string**, and a **clothespin**.
    d. Review the list of facts at the end of the lesson. Add in any additional activities or fun facts as the children show interest, but do not spend time during the lesson referring to the manual or trying to get through the list. Remember the lesson is focused on movement and imagination—the facts are intended to merely supplement the fishing activity.

2. Explain to the children that today we are going fishing to learn about what we can find in the ocean. Imagine you are in a boat, and encourage all of the children to get in and row together through the ocean. Talk about how the waves of the ocean are rocking your boat. Everyone must hold on tight so they don't fall in the water!

3. As you row out into the ocean, talk about the types of fish you will be catching today! Since the categories Live/sleep and Talk are similar between ocean animals, these will not be areas you spend time on today, so very briefly cover them here by asking:
    a. Where do all of these fish live? Can we see them? Why not? (They are all under the water.)
    b. Listen! Can anyone hear any fish? What are we listening for? Do fish bark like dogs? Do they roar like lions? Why do you think we can't hear them?
    c. Talk about how fish cannot make the same kinds of noises underwater that other animals make. They may blow bubbles or send signals to each other in other ways.

4. While you still have the children's attention, arrive at your fishing station (**sheet**). Give a child the **fishing pole** and help him get the clothespin at the end of the pole over the sheet. While the children and you stay in the imaginary boat, have another parent go behind the sheet and attach one of the **ocean animal cutouts** to the clothespin. When the child pulls the fishing pole back, have him hold up the picture for everyone to see. Together, act out the different ways these animals move, supplementing with the fun facts below as needed. Allow each child to take at least one turn with the fishing pole. (Feel free to do more as attention spans permit.)
    a. Fish: Make fishy faces and pretend to have gills to breathe through. Swim through the air together making fishy faces.
    b. Sharks: Pretend to look for smaller fish to chomp with your big shark teeth, or pretend to swim through the water holding your hand up like a dorsal fin.
    c. Whales: Take the group outside and then practice spitting water out of your mouths like a whale spout.
    d. Crabs: Practice a sideways crab walk.
    e. Jellyfish: Have the children attach themselves to each other to get free rides through the water or take turns pretending to sting each other.
    f. Blowfish: Pretend to blow up and become spiky when danger comes near.

5. Remember to go at the children's pace and allow them to have fun with this activity. Giving a new child a turn with the fishing pole is a great way to redirect their attention and get them excited about each new ocean animal!

6. After talking about each ocean animal, have the children throw their animal back into the ocean (over the sheet).

FUN FACTS (to supplement the activities above)
1. Fun facts: fish
    a. Eat: They eat smaller fish and small plants.
    b. Live/sleep: The live underwater.
    c. Move: they swim with their *fins*. Fish travel together in schools! (Optional: Talk about how we are together in a school just like fish have schools, but fish schools are for a different purpose. Talk about the differences.)
    d. Talk: Fish do not talk to each other. They do blow bubbles.
    e. Fun fact: Fish breathe through gills and the sides of their heads, and they breathe water instead of air. Just like we cannot breathe water, fish cannot breathe air. They need to live in the water to survive.

2. Fun facts: sharks
    a. Eat: Sharks eat smaller fish. Sharks can have up to eight rows of teeth! (Optional: When sharks' teeth break off, they grow new ones.)
    b. Live/sleep: Sharks live in the water. No one actually knows if sharks ever go to sleep. (Optional: Some people think that sharks only relax instead of sleeping because they still keep swimming. How would you like it if you never had to go to sleep?)
    c. Move: Sharks use their tail fins to move through the water (show the children on the cutout). They use their side fins to brake and to lift them up in the water.
    d. Talk: Sharks cannot talk.
    e. Fun fact: Sharks have a *dorsal fin* that keeps them steady in the water as they swim. (Show the children the dorsal fin on the shark cutout.)

3. Fun facts: starfish
    a. Eat: They eat smaller, slow fish.
    b. Live/sleep: They live under the water, sometimes on the floor of the ocean. (Optional: What is the *ocean floor*?)
    c. Move: Starfish have tubes on their feet, like suction cups, that can help them move around.
    d. Talk: Starfish cannot talk.
    e. Fun fact: When another fish attacks a starfish, the starfish can just let go of one of its arms!

4. Fun facts: whales
    a. Eat: Whales eat a variety of fish and other ocean animals, like octopus.
    b. Live/sleep: They live in the ocean. Like sharks, they don't really go to sleep—they just swim slower than normal to rest. (Optional: How would you like it if you never had to go to sleep?)
    c. Move: Whales swim using flippers.

d. Talk: Some whales "sing" to find other whales. They can sing for more than half an hour. Other whales whistle or click their tongues! (Optional: Whales can be very noisy—even louder than a ship's horn!)
   e. Fun fact: Whales are one of the few ocean animals that breathe air instead of water. They have a hole on top of their head called a *spout that they breathe through and spit water out of.

5. Fun facts: crabs
   a. Eat: Crabs eat plants and small animals.
   b. Live/sleep: They live in the water. Some crabs like the "shallow end" of the ocean, while others like living in deep water.
   c. Move: Some crabs move forward, backward, or sideways with their legs. (Optional: Have the children pretend to get out of the boat and practice walking like crabs. You can also have crab walk races.)
   d. Talk: Crabs don't talk, but they have big claws that can snap at others. (Optional: Have everyone pretend to snap his claws.)
   e. Fun fact: Crabs have six legs and two claws.

6. Fun facts: jellyfish
   a. Eat: They eat ocean plants and other small fish. (Optional: They can reach out with their *tentacles and sting the animals they want to eat.
   b. Live/sleep: They like to sit at the bottom of the "shallow end" of the ocean to save their energy for eating.
   c. Move: They can swim, or they attach themselves to something else in the water that is moving. They like getting free rides.
   d. Talk: Jellyfish cannot talk.
   e. Fun fact: Jellyfish have no brains. Jellyfish are made up of a Jell-O-like material!

7. Fun facts: blowfish
   a. Eat: Blowfish eat small fish, plants, crabs, and shrimp.
   b. Live/sleep: They live in the ocean.
   c. Move: They swim through the water, but they are not very good swimmers, so they have to find different ways of defending themselves. (See fun fact below.)
   d. Talk: These fish do not talk.
   e. Fun fact: When blowfish feel threatened, they gulp in a bunch of water and blow their bodies up to stick out their spikes so other fish can't eat them.

Hands-on Activity: Fish sorting

Skill: pre-math

Use the cutouts from the **Lesson 9 Images** to create two different sizes and three different colors of the each image. Allow the children to work together and sort the images by shape, size, and color. (For a faster option, buy multicolored baked fish crackers, and have the children sort them into colors.) Sorting is a pre-math skill, so this will likely be an advanced concept to them at first. Be patient and give them a lot of encouragement and assistance.

Lesson 9 Outing and Parental Supplement

Outing: The Aquarium

Skills: curiosity, gross motor, sensory development, social-emotional development

Take a trip to an aquarium if there is one available in your area. If there are none in your area, you can also go to a local Cabela's, Bass Pro Shop, pet store, or fishpond where you can watch fish swim. Talk about the facts the children learned in their lesson. How are the fish built so they can swim and breathe underwater? What are they eating? Are they awake or asleep?

Parental Supplement

Books

- *Amazing Animal Facts: A Visual Guide to the World's Most Incredible Creatures* by Jacqui Bailey
- *The Pout-Pout Fish* by Deborah Diesen
- *The Fish Who Cried Wolf* by Julia Donaldson
- *A Fish Out of Water* by P.D. Eastman
- *If You Want to See a Whale* by Julie Fogliano
- *Peanut Butter and Jellyfish* by Jarrett J. Krosoczka
- *Swimmy* by Leo Lionni
- *The Rainbow Fish* by Marcus Pfister
- *Crabby Crab* by Chris Raschka
- *Little Clam* by Lynn Reiser
- *One Fish, Two Fish, Red Fish, Blue Fish* by Dr. Seuss
- *Oxford First Book of Animals* by Barbara Taylor

Activities

- If you did not do so already for your outing, visit a local pond and see how many fish you can see. See the discussion items from the outing portion.
- Make fish faces at each other and in the mirror. Expect lots of laughter!
- If your family likes to fish, take your child on a fishing trip.
- When your child takes a bath or goes swimming, have him splash around pretending to be different ocean animals of his choice. Allow him to use his imagination and direct his own play!
- Buy some multicolored baked fish crackers and practice sorting again. Enjoy a snack together after.
- Look through books or encyclopedias to learn about some of the ocean animals not covered in this lesson or review ones that your child is excited about from the lesson.

Discussion

- Talk about where the ocean is. Look at a globe or a map. Point out where you live and how far the ocean is. Some fish can live in lakes or rivers, and some can only live in the ocean. Talk about the differences between salt water and fresh water.
- What are your child's favorite ocean animals, and what does he like best about them?
- Talk about water safety. Enforce that while fish can breathe underwater, humans can't. Review your family's safety rules for being around water.
- Safety Note: When playing with your children in water, or doing the above activities in the bathtub, parents should never leave children in the bathtub or by the swimming pool alone. Watch them constantly around water. The American Academy of Pediatrics recommends that children be at arm's length of their caregivers at all times when in or around water.

Resources Used by Authors
http://eol.org
www.clker.com
http://www.healthychildren.org/English/health-issues/injuries-emergencies/Pages/Drowning.aspx
http://www.elasmo-research.org/education/topics/b_sleep.htm
http://marinelife.about.com/od/invertebrates/tp/seastarfacts.htm
http://www.scientificamerican.com/article/how-do-whales-and-dolphin/
http://seaworld.org/en/animal-info/animal-infobooks/beluga-whales/
http://seaworld.org/en/animal-info/animal-infobooks/killer-whale/
http://nmlc.org/2009/04/how-do-whales-breathe/
http://oceanexplorer.noaa.gov/explorations/02alaska/background/crabs/crabs.html
http://www.jellywatch.org/blooms/facts
http://www.nature.org/ourinitiatives/regions/northamerica/unitedstates/indiana/journeywithnature/freshwater-jellyfish.xml
http://animals.nationalgeographic.com/animals/fish/pufferfish/
Amazing Animal Facts by Jacqui Bailey

Unit 2: Things That Are Alive
Lesson 10: Bugs

Lesson Objective: Learn more about several different bugs (insects, arachnids, etc.) in a fun and interactive environment.

Lesson 10 Skill Objectives:

- Attention span
- Creativity
- Curiosity
- Fine motor
- Gross motor
- Imaginative play
- Initiative
- Music appreciation
- Patience
- Respect
- Self-esteem
- Sensory development
- Social-emotional development
- Taking turns
- Visual tracking
- Vocabulary

Preparation

Transition Activity Materials:
- LMG SUGGESTED SONG LIST

Lesson Materials:
- Fake bugs (found at craft stores or dollar stores)
- Lesson 10 Images
- Crayons

Hands-on Activity Materials:
- Pipe cleaners (from craft stores)
- Tin foil
- Yarn

Parent Responsibility:
- Magnifying glass
- Headband

Lesson 10 Outline

1. Welcome music/gather to carpets

2. Welcome song: "The More We Get Together"

3. Attention grabber: Hocus Pocus, Everybody Focus!
   Skill: visual tracking

4. Calendar time
   Skills: patience, taking turns

5. Story time: *Some Bugs* by Angela DiTerlizzi
   Skill: attention span

6. Transition activity: "Eensy Weensy Spider"
   Skills: creativity, gross motor, music appreciation

7. Lesson: Bugs
   Skills: curiosity, gross motor, initiative, respect, self-esteem, vocabulary

8. Hands-on activity: Bug Antennae
   Skills: fine motor, imaginative play

9. Theme song

10. Children dismissed for free play

Lesson 10 Details

Teacher Tip

This curriculum calls for frequent nature walks, so we recommend trying a variety of locations, parks, and trails. Always allow the children to guide the discovery! Even though you may do the same type of outing a few weeks in a row, the children will have different experiences each time, and time spent exploring outdoors is incredibly valuable. Being outdoors and encouraging exploration is one of the core principles of the Live Move Grow program!

Transition Activity: "Eensy Weensy Spider"

Skills: creativity, gross motor, music appreciation

Play "Eensy Weensy Spider" (#13 on the **LMG SUGGESTED SONG LIST**). This song is fun to do with a few different verses that give the spider a different adjective each time. Change your movements or actions depending on which adjective you pick (ex: the very bouncy spider or the very itchy spider).

Lesson: Bugs

Skills: curiosity, gross motor, initiative, respect, self-esteem, vocabulary

7. Before the lesson prepare the following:
    a. Hide the **fake bugs** around the room. Only hide the bugs that you plan to cover during the lesson time. (If you don't have a matching toy bug, just hide a picture of one.)
    b. Review the list of facts at the end of the lesson. Add in any additional activities or fun facts as the children show interest, but do not spend time during the lesson referring to the manual or trying to get through the list. Remember the lesson is focused on movement and imagination.

8. Give each child a turn to search around the room for a bug. You can help her find one by playing a "hot/cold game" to help her search. (Ex: Hotter means she's getting closer and colder means she's too far away). Encourage her to use her **magnifying glass** to search and then more closely inspect the bug once she finds it.
    a. When she finds one, take the bug and the group back to the mat area or table.
    b. Have them find the picture of that bug on their **Lesson 10 Images** coloring page.
    c. While they color with **crayons**, share with them a couple fun facts about that bug.
    d. Let the children bring one of the bug toys home. They may need it for supplement activities and further exploration at home.

e. Option: Create your own coloring sheets with pictures that correspond to toy bugs you already own.

FUN FACTS (to supplement the activities above)
1. Fun facts: bees
   a. Eat: They eat flower nectar and pollen.
   b. Live/sleep: They sleep in their *hive.
   c. Move: We can hear a buzzing sound as they fly. (Optional: Pretend to fly around and buzz like bees.)
   d. Talk: They use movement/dance to communicate. (Optional: Do a bee dance. Ask the children what they are communicating or telling us through their dance.)
   e. Fun fact: They make honey. (Optional: Sample some honey together.)

2. Fun facts: caterpillars
   a. Eat: They eat huge amounts of plants. (Optional: Pretend to eat lots of food.)
   b. Live/sleep: They live in trees and on leaves. Some caterpillars sleep during the day.
   c. Move: They crawl and scoot using the suction on their legs.
   d. Talk: They make vibrating sounds with their hind legs and hairs on their bodies.
   e. Fun fact: After a caterpillar goes in its cocoon for a long time, it turns into a butterfly. (Optional: pretend to be butterflies.)

3. Fun facts: mosquitoes
   a. Eat: They like to drink blood. (Gross!)
   b. Live/sleep: They live in places with a lot of water. Some sleep during the day.
   c. Move: They fly.
   d. Talk: They communicate with each other by scent and the sound of their wings.
   e. Fun fact: When a mosquito bites you, you may feel itchy. (Optional: Pretend to swat away mosquitoes.)

4. Fun facts: spiders
   a. Eat: They eat other live insects. They catch them in their webs. (Optional: Pretend to get caught in a sticky web.)
   b. Live/sleep: Spiders are found all over the world. (We don't know when they sleep.)
   c. Move: They crawl, use their webs to hang, and build webs.
   d. Talk: They "talk" by feeling each other's vibration. Most don't see very well.
   e. Fun fact: Some spiders can be *poisonous. They have eight legs. (Optional: Have the children count the legs on the spider toy or picture.)

5. Fun facts: ants

a. Eat: They eat a lot of different kinds of food. They will eat almost anything.
b. Live/sleep: They like sheltered places to live, like in the ground and in trees. They make their own *anthills and sleep inside them.
c. Move: They crawl, often times in lines following each other. (Optional: Walk in a line like ants.)
d. Talk: They communicate through scent and touch. They can make noises by rubbing their legs against their bodies.
e. Fun fact: They are strong! They can hold 100 times their weight. (Optional: Put this in context for the children. Point out something in your house that might weigh about 300 pounds (like a piano or another large piece of furniture) and point out that a child could carry that item on his back if he were as strong as an ant.

6. Fun facts: snails
    a. Eat: They eat very small items left on the ground from animals and plants.
    b. Sleep/live: They live in oceans or on land where there is a lot of *moisture*. They sleep in their shells. (Optional: pretend to hide in shells to sleep.)
    c. Move: They crawl. They are very slow!
    d. Talk: They communicate by using the smell of the *mucous* trail they leave behind them when they crawl.
    e. Fun fact: They only sleep every 2–3 days.

7. Fun facts: ladybugs
    a. Eat: They eat other insects called *aphids.
    b. Live/sleep: They sleep in small plants, fields, gardens, parks, etc. They sleep at night.
    c. Move: They can walk and fly.
    d. Talk: They communicate with their scents.
    e. Fun facts: They are usually orange or red with black spots. Like many other bugs, they have *antennae* on their heads that help them to smell, taste, and feel.

Hands-on Activity: Bug Antennae

Skill: fine motor, imaginative play

Let the children pick out their antennae colors. Wrap the bottom of the **pipe cleaner** around the **headband** and secure it by twisting. At the top of the pipe cleaner, have the children clump or bend the pipe cleaner or **tin foil** into a ball. (Each child can then bend his antennae any way he wants.) This craft won't take very long, so encourage the children to play and pretend with their new antennae. Make a giant spider web out of **yarn** and pretend to get caught. Option: They could also make some simple fuzzy caterpillars with the pipe cleaners by folding them in half.

Lesson 10 Outing and Parental Supplement

Outing: Butterfly Encounter

Skills: curiosity, gross motor, sensory development, social-emotional development

Plan an outing to the nearest butterfly encounter or bug exhibit. Be sure to remind the children to bring their magnifying glasses and wear their antennae they made. You can check the Entomological Society of America website or just search online for butterfly garden, insect collections, or entomology facilities near you. You could also visit the section of the zoo that displays bugs. You can also take a nature walk and search for bugs.

Parental Supplement

Books
- *The Very Hungry Caterpillar* by Eric Carle (or any other Eric Carle books about bugs)
- *Some Bugs* by Angela DiTerlizzi
- *I Love Bugs* by Emma Dodd
- *The Best Book of Bugs* by Claire Llewellyn
- *The House at the end of Ladybug Lane* by Elise Primavera
- *Bugs Galore* by Peter Stein
- *I Love Bugs!* by Sturges
- *Busy Bug Book* by Usborne

Activities
- Make bars from rice crisp cereal according to directions on the box. Once cool enough, have children butter their hands, then give them each a blob of the mixture to create a spider body. Give each child eight pretzel sticks (or licorice) for legs. Allow to set, and enjoy for a snack! (There are a lot of other "bug" snack options. Get creative!)
- Buy or make a bug-catching net. Go on a nature walk and try to catch some bugs. You could even make a habitat for them and care for your new pet(s).
- Use a magnifying glass to search for bugs or look at the ones you caught. (You can often get one at a dollar store, or you could try to use a plastic bag filled with water, or a clear water bottle. For imaginative play, you could just make one out of paper.)
- Use the bug antenna from this week's project and pretend to be your child's favorite bug. Add whatever other costume decor would be appropriate for the bug he chooses.
- Bury your child's new bug toy in a sensory bin (filled with sand, beans, etc.) and allow him to search for the toy.
- Start a Bug Zoo. Place a cup or bowl outside and leave a small snack in it. After a few days, go check on it and see what bugs are there now.

Discussion
- Discuss the process of a caterpillar eating a lot of food, building a cocoon, and turning into a butterfly. (Read *The Very Hungry Caterpillar* by Eric Carle.)
- What other bugs go through *metamorphosis*?
- What kind of bugs have you seen around your house and yard? Are they dangerous? Are they helpful?

Resources Used by Authors
- animalstime.com
- antark.net
- australianmuseum.net.au
- biokids.umich.edu
- www.clker.com
- honeybeesuite.com
- kids.sandiegozoo.org
- http://www.ladybug-life-cycle.com/ladybug-anatomy.html
- mothernaturenetwork.com
- pbs.org

Unit 2: Things That Are Alive
Lesson 11: Reptiles and Amphibians

Lesson Objective: Learn more about several different reptiles and amphibians in a fun and interactive environment.

Lesson 11 Skill Objectives:

- Attention span
- Creativity
- Critical thinking
- Curiosity
- Fine motor
- Following directions
- Gross motor
- Patience
- Respect
- Self-esteem
- Sensory development
- Social-emotional development
- Taking turns
- Vocabulary

Preparation

Lesson Materials:

- Cardboard box
- Picture of each of following: alligator, crocodile, snake, turtle, frog, lizard
- Lesson 11 Images
- Tape
- Tube sock
- Misc. items like stuffed animal, ball, or can of soup
- Pillow or box for each child
- Rope
- Lily pads cut out of paper
- Raisins

Hands-on Activity Materials:

- Half an egg carton for each child
- Paint
- Glue
- Googly eyes
- Red paper

Parent Responsibility:

- Send child with a shirt that can get paint on it

Lesson 11 Outline

1. Welcome music/gather to carpets

2. Welcome song: "The More We Get Together"

3. Attention grabber: One, Two, Three, Now Follow Me!
   Skill: following directions

4. Calendar time
   Skills: patience, taking turns

5. Story time: *The Mixed-Up Chameleon* by Eric Carle
   Skills: attention span, critical thinking

6. Transition activity: Leap Frog
   Skills: gross motor, patience, taking turns

7. Lesson: Reptiles and Amphibians
   Skills: gross motor, initiative, respect, self-esteem

8. Hands-on activity: Egg Carton Snakes
   Skills: creativity, fine motor

9. Theme song

10. Children dismissed for free play

Lesson 11 Details

Teacher Tip: Have Fun

As you teach, have fun with the children and the information being taught. Portray excitement and wonder about the topic you are teaching in an effort to hold the children's attention, inspire their curiosity, and support critical thinking. We believe that keeping children's natural love of learning alive is imperative for success in any educational setting. If these lesson experiences can continue to amaze, instruct, inspire, and entertain the children, their minds will be stimulated, and they will continue making connections.

Remember to avoid the fact trap of merely reciting too many facts in this lesson. Read the Teacher Tip in Lesson 7 for more details.

Transition Activity: Leap Frog

Skills: gross motor, patience, taking turns

Help one child to duck down, then assist the others in taking turns playing leap frog over each other to form a long line. Continue the line and rotate along as the last person jumps over the others, all the way to the front, each time.

Lesson: Reptiles and Amphibians

Skills: gross motor, initiative, respect, self-esteem, vocabulary

9. Before the lesson prepare the following:
   a. Create a "reptile die" (die as in "dice") using a **cardboard box** and **pictures of the following: alligator, crocodile, snake, turtle, frog, and lizard**. Put one picture on each of the die's six sides. (You can also draw the reptiles yourself.)
   b. Review the list of facts at the end of the lesson. Add in any additional activities or fun facts as the children show interest, but do not spend time during the lesson referring to the manual or trying to get through the list.

10. Begin your lesson by discussing reptiles. They are animals that are cold-blooded. This means that they use their *environment* to keep themselves at the right temperature. (Humans are not reptiles, so our blood and body stay at the right temperature mostly on their own!) Reptiles have scales on the outside of their bodies to protect them. Their skin is tougher and harder than ours. Reptiles hatch from eggs!

11. Have each child take a turn rolling the reptile die. Announce the name of the animal the die lands on.

12. While you discuss fun facts about that animal, guide the children in taking turns picking out the corresponding picture cutouts from the **Lesson 11 Images**. Help them **tape** the images on the correct side of the die. The images correspond with the animals as follows:
    a. Alligator: alligator, fish, bird, swamp
    b. Crocodile: mean, longer heads, swim
    c. Snake: mice, egg, tongues, slither
    d. Turtle: turtle, grass, shell, eggs
    e. Frog: insects, tongue, lily pad, tadpole
    f. Lizard: plants, insects, gecko, iguana

13. Once you have all the cutouts placed on the box for the animal you are discussing, do the corresponding activity for each animal.
    a. Alligator: Recite "Five Little Monkeys Swinging in a Tree."

    > Five little monkeys swinging in the tree,
    > Teasing Mr. Alligator, "Can't catch me! You can't catch me!"
    > Then along came Mr. Alligator, quiet as can be . . .
    > And SNAP!
    >
    > Four little monkeys swinging in the tree (etc.)

    Have the children be in the "tree" (on the couch) while you act like the alligator. Act out the rhyme, and each time you get to the "snap!" at the end of the verse, grab one of the children and pull him into the "water" (on the floor with you). The children who have been caught can help you sing the next verses until everyone is caught.

    b. Crocodile: Play crocodile keep-away. Have the children try and "cross a river" (the room) without the crocodile (you) getting them.
    c. Snake: Let the children pretend to feed a snake. Use a long **tube sock** as the snake and let them feed it by putting things in the sock (**a stuffed animal, a ball, a can of soup**, etc.). This shows them how snakes swallow things whole, which often leaves a big lump in their middle.
    d. Turtle: Do the turtle walk by loosely tying a **pillow or box** to each child's back using **rope**. Have the children move slowly like turtles. When they see the "crocodile" (you) coming, they have to tuck in their limbs and hide in their "shells" (under the pillow). The children can also take turns being the crocodile and chasing or hiding from each other.
    e. Frog: Do the lily pad hop. Place **lily pads cut out of paper** across the floor and have the children hop across an imaginary pond. Also have them catch "flies" (**raisins**) to eat. (For less mess, have them stick out their tongues and place raisins directly into their mouths.)

f. Lizard: Pretend to use *camouflage* like a chameleon. Have each child hide and then explain what color his body would turn in order to camouflage with his environment. (Help him decide on the color as necessary.)

14. Continue to roll the die until you have done the activity for each animal. (You might have to "help" the die land on a specific side if something isn't getting rolled!) If you roll the same animal twice, feel free to review vocabulary, facts, or activities as your group allows.

FUN FACTS (to supplement the activities above)
1. Fun facts: alligators and crocodiles
    a. Eat: They eat many different types of meat including fish, snakes, turtles, birds, and more.
    b. Live/sleep: They live in swamps, rivers, lakes, and ponds. They don't sleep like us; they just rest.
    c. Move: They are great swimmers in the water and can also crawl on four short legs on land.
    d. Talk: They make a deep rumbling sound.
    e. Fun fact: Crocodiles and alligators are very similar. The main differences are that crocodiles have longer heads, are more *aggressive,* and have lighter-colored scales.

2. Fun facts: snakes
    a. Eat: They eat meat such as insects, *rodents*, birds, eggs, and more. They swallow their food whole by opening their mouths really wide.
    b. Live/sleep: Snakes live in lots of different places like deserts, forests, and oceans. It's hard to know when a snake is sleeping because they don't have eyelids. They can't close their eyes!
    c. Move: They slither (slide) along the ground because they don't have arms and legs.
    d. Talk: They "talk" through scent and movements.
    e. Fun fact: Snakes don't have noses like we do. They stick out their tongues to smell. Some snakes are poisonous and have *fangs*.

3. Fun facts: turtles
    a. Eat: They eat grass, plants, and some small insects by snapping at their food with their beak-like mouths.
    b. Live/sleep: Some turtles live in the water while others live on land. They don't sleep like we do; they just rest.
    c. Move: They have webbed feet so they can swim better. They can also walk slowly and climb.

d. Talk: They communicate by smells and by feeling vibrations or movements.

   e. Fun fact: They lay their eggs on land.

4. Fun facts: frogs
   a. Eat: They eat live insects like flies and grasshoppers. They use their special tongues to reach out and grab their food.
   b. Live/sleep: Frogs live all around the world, but they always live near water. When it's cold outside, they go hide somewhere safe and sleep for a long time This is called *hibernation.
   c. Move: They jump and swim.
   d. Talk: They make a croaking sound.
   e. Fun fact: They are *amphibians*, which means they start their lives in the water as eggs, then become tadpoles, and finally finish growing into full frogs that live on land. This is another example of metamorphosis.

5. Fun facts: lizards
   a. Eat: They eat plants, insects, and/or fruit.
   b. Live/sleep: They live mostly in trees or rocky areas, but they like to be near water.
   c. Move: They can walk on land and also love to swim. They can stay underwater for a long time. Most lizards have four legs.
   d. Talk: They "talk" through scent and movements.
   e. Fun fact: There are many kinds of lizards, like iguanas, chameleons, and geckos. They are all unique and live all over the world!

Hands-on Activity: Egg Carton Snakes

Skills: creativity, fine motor

Cut **egg cartons** in half lengthwise ("hot dog" style) and give each child half a carton. Let the children **paint** their snakes however they choose. Place a dot of **glue** where the eyes and tongue should go, and have the children add the **googly eyes** and a tongue (cut from **red paper**).

Lesson 11 Outing and Parental Supplement

Outing: Pet Store

Skills: curiosity, gross motor, sensory development, social-emotional development

Go to a pet store that has reptiles and amphibians. Have fun observing them, and ask the children a lot of questions. Discuss fun facts about the animals.

Parental Supplement

Books:

- *Amazing Animal Facts: A Visual Guide to the World's Most Incredible Creatures* by Jacqui Bailey
- *Verdi* by Janell Cannon
- *The Mixed-Up Chameleon* by Eric Carle
- *A Color of His Own* by Leo Lionni
- *A Frog Thing* by James Muscarello
- *Alligators All Around* by Maurice Sendak
- *Yertle the Turtle* by Dr. Seuss
- *I'll Follow the Moon* by Stephanie Lisa Tara
- *Oxford First Book of Animals* by Barbara Taylor

Activities:

- Create a frog. Cut out a frog shape, picture, or coloring page. Fold a long, skinny piece of red paper several times (accordion style), and attach it to the frog's mouth. It will look like the frog's long tongue is trying to catch flies. You could use raisins for flies or make fake little flies for the frog to catch. You can also cut out some green circles with wedges to look like lily pads. Lay them out in a path across a "pond" (a blue blanket). Make the frog hop from lily pad to lily pad to get to the other side.
- If weather permits, visit the reptile or amphibian displays at the zoo.
- If applicable, visit a neighbor's pet snake, frog, or lizard.
- Use a large box as a turtle shell. Cut out pieces so arms, legs, and head can move in and out, or just strap a large pillow to your child's back. Someone pretend to be a crocodile. When the crocodile gets close, the child can curl up and hide in or under his "shell."
- Make snakes out of play dough, bread sticks, or cookie dough. Have child help roll out the dough into long "snakes." Decorate as desired.

Discussion:

- Discuss metamorphosis. Compare a tadpole to a frog vs. a caterpillar to a butterfly (from Lesson 10).

- Which animal from this lesson is your child's favorite? Why?
- Talk about safety when hiking or exploring. Some reptiles (as well as other animals and insects) are poisonous.
- Animals defend themselves so they can stay safe. How do some of the animals in this lesson defend themselves? (Ex: Chameleons change color, some snakes can rattle their tails, turtles hide in their shells, some frogs are poisonous, etc.)

Resources Used by Authors
- www.clker.com
- http://www.blogmemom.com/recycled-crafts-kids-snake-craft/
- http://www.kidzone.ws/animals/reptiles1.htm
- http://animals.pawnation.com/communication-between-snakes-5024.html
- http://www.animalstown.com/animals/t/turtle/turtle.php
- http://animals.sandiegozoo.org/animals/turtle-tortoise
- http://www.gulfturtles.com/when-do-turtles-sleep
- http://animalquestions.org/reptiles/alligators/do-alligators-hibernate/
- http://www.sciencekids.co.nz/sciencefacts/animals/crocodilealligatordifferences.html
- http://animals.nationalgeographic.com
- http://factzoo.com

Unit 2: Things That Are Alive
Lesson 12: Birds

Lesson Objective: Learn more about birds and bats.

Lesson 12 Skill Objectives:

- Attention span
- Curiosity
- Fine motor
- Following directions
- Gratitude
- Gross motor
- Imaginative play
- Patience
- Respect
- Self-esteem
- Sensory development
- Social-emotional development
- Taking turns
- Teamwork
- Vocabulary

Preparation

Transition Activity Materials:

- Several plastic eggs

Lesson Materials:

- Pictures of birds, bats, and penguins (optional)
- Gathered branches (to build a nest)
- Gummy worms (optional)
- Blankets
- Chairs

Hands-on Activity Materials:

- Craft feathers (optional)
- Lesson 12 Images
- Brown pipe cleaners
- Red, orange, and yellow paper
- Scissors
- Glue
- Googly eyes

Parental Responsibility:

- Ask parents ahead of time if children can wade in water during penguin habitat portion of lesson
- Ask a parent to come early for pick-up to help with the hands-on activity
- Toilet paper roll for their child

Lesson 12 Outline

1. Welcome music/gather to carpets

2. Welcome song: "The More We Get Together"

3. Attention grabber: Do What I'm Doing
   Skills: following directions, gross motor

4. Calendar time
   Skills: patience, taking turns

5. Story time: *Are You My Mother?* by P.D. Eastman
   Skill: attention span

6. Transition activity: Egg Hunt
   Skills: teamwork, patience

7. Lesson: Birds of a Feather
   Skills: curiosity, gross motor, imaginative play

8. Hands-on activity: Thanksgiving Turkey Craft
   Skills: fine motor, gratitude

9. Theme song

10. Children dismissed for free play

Lesson 12 Details

Teacher Tip: Make Connections

Strive to create teachable moments wherein the children can make connections. To facilitate critical thinking, don't ask yes or no questions; instead, ask why, how, etc. If they don't know the answer, that is absolutely all right (and to be expected!). Try to guide them toward answers or allow time for the children to process information. They might surprise you! When reading a book, take time to stop, ask these types of great questions, and apply the story to the children whenever possible.

Remember to avoid the fact trap of merely reciting too many facts in this lesson. Read the Teacher Tip in Lesson 7 for more details.

Transition Activity: Egg Hunt

Skills: teamwork, patience

Before the lesson, hide several **plastic eggs** around the room. Once the children have found them, play another round in which a child hides the eggs for the others to find. When the children are done with this activity, use the eggs to lead into the lesson about bird habitats. (Ex: "These eggs need a place to go! Where do we find eggs in nature? Should we build the eggs a nest?")

Lesson: Birds of a Feather

Skills: gross motor, initiative, respect, self-esteem, vocabulary

1. Gather the children on their mats and tell them, "Today, you will be traveling to several places to see where different kinds of birds live. In each of those places, you will learn about the bird or animal that lives there!"

2. For each of the animals listed below, have the children help you to create a habitat. As you sit or stand in the habitat, learn more fun facts about each animal.
    a. On your way to build each new habitat, move like the bird you are discussing: fly like birds and bats and waddle like penguins.
    b. Optional: Feel free to have **pictures of birds, bats, and penguins** to show the children as you are discussing the animals.

3. Bird habitat

a. Find a safe place that is off the floor, like the couch, stacked couch cushions, or the kitchen table. (Safety note: Please make sure that you are not anywhere that the children could fall and hurt themselves.)
b. Create a nest from **gathered branches**. (Monitor the branches closely to ensure no one gets scratched or hurt.) You can also pretend to make a nest from imaginary branches.
c. Talk about how most birds live in trees. Pretend that you are *perched* in a tree. Imagine what it looks like all around you, and talk about what you see down below. Discuss the fun facts about birds listed below, and discuss how you would like living like a bird.
d. Optional: Scatter **gummy worms** and tell the children they must hunt for worms like birds do. Have fun snacking on the gummy worms.

4. Bat habitat
    a. Bats are not birds, but they also have wings, and they can fly!
    b. Have the children help you build a pretend cave (fort) out of **blankets** and **chairs**. Talk about caves and how they are dark, damp, and cold. Make sure the cave fort is big enough to hold everyone.
    c. Once you have built your cave, climb inside, and review the facts about bats listed below. Discuss how bats live.
    d. Optional: Have the children practice hanging upside down by putting their feet up on the couch. How would they like living like bats?

5. Penguin habitat
    a. Penguins are birds, but they don't fly. They live in cold places and spend a lot of time in the water.
    b. Fill a bathtub or a kiddie pool with a small amount of water. Have the children stand in it and pretend to be penguins. (Make sure only their feet get wet. They can roll up their pants and take off their socks and shoes, but this should not be an activity that will require a change of clothes. Explain to the children beforehand that there should be no splashing each other with water.)
    c. Safety note: Please ensure that the children don't slip in the water. Do not leave them unsupervised under any circumstances. If any of the parents are uncomfortable with water, you could stand in an empty bathtub or kiddie pool and pretend there is water.
    d. Discuss some facts about penguins! How would the children like to live like penguins?
    e. Optional: Add a few ice cubes to the water! Talk about how penguins swim in extremely cold water. (If using ice cubes, do not allow the children to stay in the water for more than a few minutes.)

FUN FACTS (to supplement the habitat activity above)
1. Fun facts: birds (general)
    a. Eat: They eat seeds, worms, and bugs. Some bigger birds even eat fish.
    b. Live/sleep: They build nests for their homes and to lay their eggs in, and they live and sleep in trees.
    c. Move: They fly.
    d. Talk: "Chirp chirp," "Caw caw," and "Whooooo" (owls).
    e. Fun fact: Birds have wings and feathers to help them fly. Their feathers only last for one year. When they all fall out, birds grow new feathers.

2. Fun facts: bats
    a. Eat: Bats eat small animals, bugs, fish, or fruit.
    b. Live/sleep: Bats mostly live in caves during the day, and they like to hunt for food at night. They sleep hanging upside down by their feet!
    c. Move: They can fly even though they aren't actually birds. (They don't have feathers.)
    d. Talk: Bats scream at such a high *pitch* that we can't even hear them.
    e. Fun fact: Bats know where to go because their sense of hearing is so good! (Review sense of hearing from Unit 1.) Instead of looking with their eyes, bats make high-pitched noises and then listen for other sounds to know where to go.

3. Fun facts: penguins
    a. Eat: Penguins eat fish that they catch while they are swimming.
    b. Live/sleep: They live in Antarctica where it is very, very cold.
    c. Move: They like to waddle around on their feet or swim in the cold water.
    d. Talk: They call to each other (make loud noises) and also do different actions with their bodies (like flapping their wings or stomping their feet) to tell each other things or warn each other of danger.
    e. Fun fact: Penguins have wings, which makes them birds, but instead of flying like most birds, they use their wings like flippers to swim in the water.

Hands-on Activity: Thanksgiving Turkey Craft

Skills: fine motor, gratitude

Note: This craft will be easier if you have help, so consider asking parents to come early for pick-up. If no one is available, consider pre-cutting the hands (or using **craft feathers** instead of paper) and marking the toilet paper rolls where the eyes, nose, and wattle (red neck piece) should be glued.

1. Before the children arrive, use **Lesson 12 Images** as a template to cut out noses from orange paper and wattles from red paper. Cut the **brown pipe cleaner** and bend to look like turkey feet (three toes and room at the top to glue to the toilet paper roll).

2. Have each child trace her hands (with assistance) on **red, orange and yellow paper**, then have an adult cut them out with **scissors**.

3. Stand the **toilet paper roll** up on the table. **Glue** the hand cutouts to the back of the toilet paper roll to represent the turkey feathers. Glue the **googly eyes**, beak, and wattle to the front of the toilet paper roll to make a turkey face. (It may help if you place the dots of glue where the parts of the turkey's face should go. The children can then add the pieces on their own.) Finally, glue the feet to the inside front of the toilet paper roll.

4. As you work on your craft, talk about the things each child is grateful for. Encourage them to say thank you for these things.

Lesson 12 Outing and Parental Supplement

Outing: Aviary

Skills: curiosity, gross motor, sensory development, social-emotional development

Observe birds at an aviary. If there are no aviaries in your area, take an outdoor walk and look for birds, go to a nearby duck pond, visit a pet store, or find a friend with pet birds.

Parental Supplement

Books:

- *Amazing Animal Facts: A Visual Guide to the World's Most Incredible Creatures* by Jacqui Bailey
- *Stellaluna* by Janell Cannon
- *Have You Heard the Nesting Bird?* by Rita Gray
- *Tacky the Penguin* by Helen Lester
- *Oxford First Book of Animals* by Barbara Taylor
- *Owl Moon* by Jane Yolen

Activities:

- Talk about how birds need to have good balance. Set up a "branch" (a 2x4, rope, tape, etc. on the ground). Pretend to fly around the room and land on the "branch."
- Flamingos have good balance too. Stand on one leg like a flamingo. Put some snacks on a short table, chair, or box. Have your child stand on one leg, bend down and try to eat her snack without falling over. (She may need help!)
- Hummingbirds eat nectar from flowers. Put a small amount of water or juice in some cups and place them around the room. (You could even tape some fake petals around the rim of the cup.) Have your child pretend to fly around the room holding a straw in her mouth looking for flowers. Let her drink the "nectar" from each "flower."
- Play "Is It a Bird?" Ask your child if something is a bird (duck, chicken, bee, airplane, etc.). Ask why it is or is not a bird (wings, feathers, it flies, beak, etc.).
- Go for a walk together, and look for different types of birds. Talk about their sizes, shapes, and colors. Talk about the different noises they make. How do we know that they are birds? Practice looking and listening for birds by using your homemade binoculars from Lesson 2. If it's too cold to go for a walk, look out a window. (You can do this activity in a car.) How many birds can you see? Practice counting.
- Make a homemade bird feeder together. For a simple feeder, cover a pinecone in peanut butter and birdseed. Put your feeder outside your window and watch for birds.
- Since only a few different types of birds or flying animals were covered in this week's lesson, your child might enjoy looking up information on all kinds of different birds.

Discussion:
- Discuss the process of eggs being laid, birds sitting on their eggs, and the eggs hatching.
- Talk about how differently birds live than we do. Ask your child, "What would you like about being a bird? What would you not like about being a bird?"
- Discuss the difference between humans and birds. Birds have wings that help them to fly, but because we do not have wings, we cannot fly. We should not try to fly off of high places because we could get hurt.
- Out of all of the birds we have seen and talked about, which one is your child's favorite and why?
- Why do you think people describe the sound birds make as "singing?" Does it sound like singing to you?
- As you admire her Thanksgiving craft, discuss things that you are grateful for and talk about Thanksgiving.

Resources Used by Authors
- http://eol.org/
- http://www.humanesociety.org/animals/resources/tips/feeding_birds.html
- http://seaworld.org/en/animal-info/animal-infobooks/penguin/communication/
- http://www.whatdobirdseat.info/

Unit 2: Things That Are Alive
Lesson 13: You Are Alive—Parts of the Body

Lesson Objective: Help children learn about their own bodies and what they are capable of.

Lesson 13 Skill Objectives:

- Attention span
- Decision making
- Expressive language
- Fine motor
- Following directions
- Gross motor
- Healthy habits
- Music appreciation
- Patience
- Positive self-image
- Self-esteem
- Social-emotional development
- Taking turns

Preparation

Transition Activity Materials:

- LMG SUGGESTED SONG LIST

Lesson Materials:

- Stethoscope (optional)
- Small toys

Hands-on Activity Materials:

- Printouts from Lesson 13 Images
- Stapler
- Tape
- Coloring materials
- Glue sticks

Parental Responsibility:

- Picture of child brought from home (optional)

Lesson 13 Outline

1. Welcome music/gather to carpets

2. Welcome song: "The More We Get Together"

3. Attention grabber: Stand Up, Sit Down.
   Skills: following directions, gross motor

4. Calendar time
   Skills: patience, taking turns

5. Story time: *From Head to Toe* by Eric Carle
   Skill: attention span

6. Transition activity: "Head, Shoulders, Knees, and Toes"
   Skills: gross motor, music appreciation

7. Lesson: Parts of the Body
   Skills: gross motor, positive self-image, self-esteem

8. Hands-on activity: All about Me
   Skills: decision making, fine motor, self-esteem

9. Theme song

10. Children dismissed for free play

Lesson 13 Details

Teacher Tip: Build Confidence through Coloring

Coloring is a great activity for preschoolers. It is a way for them to improve fine motor strength (needed for writing), increase creativity, and build confidence in their artistic expression. Anytime children are drawing or crafting, instead of asking, "What is that?" you should say, "Tell me about what you made!" This will encourage their self-esteem as you validate their creation—after all, their representation is real and accurate in their mind. Also remember that children of this age show varied amounts of interest in coloring. Never force a child to participate in an activity, but instead encourage participation for a reasonable amount of time.

Transition Activity: "Head, Shoulders, Knees, and Toes"

Skills: gross motor, music appreciation

Get the students up and moving by playing "Head, Shoulders, Knees, and Toes" (#14 on the **LMG SUGGESTED SONG LIST**).

Lesson: My Body Is Alive

Skills: gross motor, initiative, respect, self-esteem, vocabulary

1. Introduce the lesson
    a. Feel free to have fun and be silly during this lesson. This will capture their attention and curiosity about what you are teaching.
    b. Ask, "What are some of the living things we have learned about in the last several weeks?" Allow the children to talk about some of their favorites.
    c. Reinforce that each of these animals is alive. Say, "We know they are alive because they can eat, sleep, move, and talk, and so can we! We have amazing bodies that allow us to do all of these things, and today we will learn more about what our bodies can do!"
    d. Discuss the following parts of our bodies and what they can do.

2. Head
    a. Discussion: Our head holds our brain. Can we see our brains? They are inside our heads, and we cannot see them, but they help us to think!
    b. Activity: Place hands on head to demonstrate where the brain is. Have the students close their eyes and think of something they like to do. Have them tap on their heads and say with you, "Think, think, think!" Then have each child open his eyes and take turns telling you what he was thinking about.

3. Hair
    a. Discussion: We all have different colors of hair. What animals have we learned about that have hair? How is their hair different from the hair we have?
    b. Activity: Observe the colors of hair in the class.

4. Eyes
    a. Discussion: We all have different colors of eyes. What can we do with our eyes? How hard would it be if we could not see?
    b. Activity: Ask each child to tell you what color his eyes are. Demonstrate blinking.
    c. Optional: Blindfold a child and ask him to try walking across the room without being able to see. Discuss how grateful we are to have eyes.

5. Nose
    a. Discussion: What can our noses do?
    b. Activity: Sniff. Talk about what you smell. Wrinkle or wiggle your noses.

6. Mouth
    a. Discussion: What can our mouths do? (Eat, talk, whistle, etc.)
    b. Activity: Try talking without opening your mouth. Make funny faces.

7. Ears
    a. Discussion: How many ears do we have? What do they do?
    b. Activity: Try talking to each other with ears plugged.

8. Chest
    a. Discussion: Where is your chest? What is inside it?

9. Heart
    a. Discussion: Our beating heart is what keeps us alive. It goes faster when we are moving more. Our hearts go, "Thump, thump."
    b. Activity: To represent the heart's motion to the children, clench and relax your hand while saying, "Thump, thump." Have the children do it too. Have everyone jump up and down for 30 seconds and then put their hands on their chests and feel their heart beating!
    c. Optional: If you have access to a **stethoscope**, let the children take turns listening to each other's hearts. (You can also make a simple stethoscope at home.)

10. Lungs
    a. Discussion: Our lungs help us breathe. They are like big balloons inside our chest that blow up when we breathe.

b. Activity: Take deep breaths together and show the children how your chest rises when you breathe. Lie down on your backs, place a **small toy** or other item on everyone's chest, and watch the toys rise and fall as you breathe deeply.

11. Arms and hands
    a. Discussion: What can we do with our arms and hands? Can an elephant do the same things with his arms and hands? Can a monkey?
    b. Activity: Wave to each other. Try carrying a few things around the room. Give hugs. Clap. Pretend to cook, play piano, color, etc.

12. Legs and feet
    a. Discussion: What can we do with our legs and feet?
    b. Activity: Walk, march, jump, stomp, run, and skip!

13. Bones
    a. Discussion: Bones are the hard parts of our body that help us stand up straight.
    b. Activity: Have everyone find the hard parts of their arms, legs, face, or back.

14. Muscles
    a. Discussion: Muscles make us strong enough to move and be active.
    b. Activity: Have the students flex their arms. Show them where their muscles are. Make tough bodybuilder noises as you flex your muscles. Have fun!

15. Skin
    a. Discussion: Where is our skin? Why do we have skin? (To hold all of our insides in place and protect our bodies.)
    b. Activity: Have everyone touch his own skin.

16. Conclude by saying, "Each of our bodies is unique! We can do many things with our bodies because we are alive. Our bodies look different from each other. We can be so grateful for our bodies and all of the amazing things that they can do!"

Hands-on Activity: All about Me

Skills: decision making, fine motor, self-esteem

Before the activity, assemble the booklets (from **Chapter 13 Images**) by **stapling** the books together and then **taping** the fronts and backs of the pages so they turn easily. During class, explain that the children will make books all about themselves. Ask each child the questions in the book, and write in their answers. Have them decorate their books with **coloring materials**. Encourage them to exercise their fine motor skills through coloring, drawing, and circling. Encourage them to take their books home to show their families!

Optional: On page 2, glue in a **picture of each child brought from home**. On page 3 (numbers 3–5) parents can take pictures of their child doing the activities and glue them in later. (Children can also simply draw themselves doing the activities.) On page 6, have children circle the picture of their favorite body part.

Lesson 13 Outing and Parental Supplement

Outing: Picnic

Skills: expressive language, following directions, gross motor, healthy habits, social-emotional development

Have a picnic somewhere that has room to run. (If you need to be inside because of the weather, consider a gymnasium.) As you eat, remind them that eating is an important part of being alive. Let the children decide what to talk about during the picnic, and remind them that talking is also part of being alive. After eating, play an active game that requires a lot of running and movement. Give the children a few choices, but let them decide what to do. Remind them that that their bodies are amazing; they are able to run, jump, and move because they are alive. Finally, lie down together on a blanket. Talk about how being alive means we need to rest so our bodies can be ready to jump, move, and run again.

Parental Supplement

Books:

- *The Skeleton Inside You* by Philip Balenstrino (advanced)
- *From Head to Toe* by Eric Carle
- *The Magic School Bus inside the Human Body* by Joanna Cole (advanced)
- *Here Are My Hands* by Bill Martin Jr. and John Archambault
- *The Busy Body Book: A Kid's Guide to Fitness* by Lizzy Rockwell

Activities:

- Take pictures of your child doing the different activities listed in his book and add those photos to his "All about Me" book.
- Spend time practicing different things that our bodies can do.
- Sing "Head, Shoulders, Knees, and Toes" and do the actions.
- Jump on a trampoline.
- Have your child lie down on butcher paper, and trace his body. You can then draw or color on the outline as you review body parts.
- Blow up balloons and talk about how lungs work.
- Have a staring contest. After someone blinks, talk about how important it is to close our eyes sometimes. It feels good to sleep, and our bodies need sleep to grow, heal, etc.

Discussion:

- As frequently as you can, point out what body part a child is using when performing a certain task or moving from place to place.
- At mealtime, talk about how all living things have to eat. Talk about how it's important to give our bodies the energy they need.

- At bedtime, talk about how all living things need rest. Our bodies need to sleep to stay strong. (This will be a good lead-in to next week's lesson about taking care of our bodies.)
- Continue to point out and discuss ways that each of our bodies is unique. Talk about the differences in your family. Some people are taller and some are shorter. Some have blonde hair and some have brown. What other differences can you find? What similarities are there?
- Talk about gratitude for our bodies and all of the things they allow us to do. Ask your child to think about the parts of his body he is most grateful for. Ask him why he feels this way.
- Talk about the differences in human bodies and different animal bodies that we have learned about in this unit.

Resources Used by Authors
- www.clker.com

Unit 2: Things That Are Alive
Lesson 14: You Are Alive—My Healthy Body

Lesson Objective: Teach the children that it is important to take care of our amazing bodies, which are alive.

Lesson 14 Skill Objectives:

- Attention span
- Creativity
- Critical thinking
- Decision making
- Fine motor
- Following directions
- Gross motor

- Healthy habits
- Patience
- Resourcefulness
- Sensory development
- Social-emotional development
- Taking turns
- Teamwork

Preparation

Transition Activity Materials:

- Music (optional)

Lesson Materials:

- Food (real, pretend, or pictures)
- Large mixing bowl
- Small mixing bowl
- Paper plate
- Pink paint or paper
- Red marker or crayon

- Glue
- Small white objects (pom poms, beads, beans, etc.)
- New, inexpensive toothbrush
- String or floss
- Colored glitter

Hands-on Activity Materials:

- Several fruits or vegetable cut in half (carrots, potatoes, celery, apples, etc.)
- Washable paints

- Paper

Lesson 14 Outline

1. Welcome music/gather to carpets

2. Welcome song: "The More We Get Together"

3. Attention grabber: Hands on Top, That Means Stop!
   Skill: following directions

4. Calendar time
   Skills: patience, taking turns

5. Story time: *I Will Never Not Ever Eat a Tomato* by Lauren Child
   Skill: attention span

6. Transition activity: Exercises
   Skills: following directions, gross motor, healthy habits

7. Lesson: My Healthy Body
   Skills: critical thinking, decision making, fine motor, gross motor, healthy habits

8. Hands-on activity: Vegetable Stamps
   Skills: creativity, resourcefulness

9. Theme song

10. Children dismissed for free play

Lesson 14 Details

Teacher Tip: Create an Atmosphere of Respect

When children answer questions or volunteer to participate, they can raise their hand before they share. This will encourage respect for the teacher, self-confidence in their knowledge, self-control of their actions, and the initiative to share thoughts. Also, remember to review your class rules that were created at the beginning of the program. It is important to reinforce the responsibility the children have to obey the rules and respect the teacher.

Transition Activity: Exercises

Skills: following directions, gross motor, healthy habits

It is important to allow children to move because it is an essential part of their development. Try the following movements with them: hop on one foot, summersault, touch opposite arm to opposite toe, and do jumping jacks.

Lesson: My Healthy Body

Skills: critical thinking, decision making, fine motor, gross motor, healthy habits

1. Teach the children that we can be healthy in a lot of ways! Explain that today we will focus on eating healthy, brushing and flossing our teeth, and washing our hands and bodies.

2. Eating healthy
   a. Discussion: What are healthy foods? Things like fruits, vegetables, meats, breads, and dairy are healthy. Unhealthy foods have high amounts of sugar and fat that are not good for our bodies. When we eat too many unhealthy foods, we can feel tired and yucky. When we eat a lot of healthy foods, our bodies can feel good, strong, and happy!
   b. Activity: Sort food to help the children learn which foods are healthy or unhealthy. Have several examples of food (you can use **real food, pretend food, or even pictures**). Take turns sorting the foods into **large and small mixing bowls**. (Choose bowls that have very different sizes to demonstrate your point.) Healthy foods (like fruits, vegetables, and breads) go in the large bowl, and unhealthy foods (like sugar, butter, and candy) go in the small bowl. Explain that we want to eat lots of healthy food, and only small *portions* of unhealthy foods.

3. Brushing and flossing teeth

a. Discussion: We need to keep our teeth clean and healthy so that we can chew, smile, and talk! We do this by brushing everything off of our teeth and cleaning in between our teeth with floss.
b. Activity: Clean the Mouth
   i. Beforehand, make the "mouth." (Depending on your class's needs, you can decide whether to make one for each child or just take turns with one.) Cover your **paper plate** with **pink paint or paper**. Fold your pink paper plate in half. Unfold it. Draw a tongue in the middle of the bottom half with a **red marker or crayon**. Along the top and bottom edge **glue** 10 **small white objects** (like white beans, pom poms, marshmallows, etc.). This should give you 20 total "teeth," which is how many teeth the preschoolers should have right now.
   ii. Use a **toothbrush** to show the children the proper way to brush, brushing slowly on all the sides of the teeth and along the gumline in circular motions. (No water or toothpaste is recommended for this activity.) Allow the children to take turns brushing the mouth.
   iii. Use **string or floss** to demonstrate proper flossing (gently hugging the floss along the sides of the teeth and not just going straight up and down).
   iv. Optional: Loosely attach some "food" to the mouth that needs to be brushed and flossed away. You could use play dough, quilt batting, or anything else you have on hand for this activity.

4. Washing hands and bodies
   a. Discussion: There are tiny things called *germs that can make us sick. They like to hide in all kinds of places. Our hands can get germs on them, so it's important to wash our hands. It is especially important to wash our hands after we go to the bathroom and also before we eat. Our bodies get dirty too, and that is why we need to bathe.
   b. Activity: Play with glitter germs. Go to a bathroom or the kitchen, and get one child's hands damp with water. Pour some **glitter** on her hands and rub it around. Explain that all the little glitters are pretend germs. Then have the child shake hands or give high fives to the other classmates and watch how easily "germs" are spread. When you're done, help the students wash their hands.

Hands-on Activity: Vegetable Stamps

Skills: creativity, resourcefulness

Allow the children to create art by dipping the **vegetables and fruits cut in half** into **washable paint** and stamping them onto **paper**. Carrots, potatoes, celery, and apples work great for this activity.

Lesson 14 Outing and Parental Supplement

Outing: Sous-Chefs

Skills: friendship/social-emotional development, healthy habits, sensory development, teamwork

Pick an easy, healthy recipe for the group to make, like fruit salad, vegetable soup, or homemade pizza. Make a shopping list together and have a copy for each child to hold. Go on a shopping trip together, and allow the children to do as much as possible: push carts, hold the list, check off the list, pick the produce, etc. Return to someone's house and make the recipe. Again, allow the children to be heavily involved (ex: cut bananas, de-vine grapes, mix, dump, etc.). Enjoy your finished product together!

Parental Supplement

Books:

- *I Will Never Not Ever Eat a Tomato* by Lauren Child
- *The Healthy Body Cookbook* by Joan D'Amico and Karen Eich Drummond
- *Dudley: The Little Terrier That Could* by Stephen Green-Armytage
- *Shhhh! Everybody's Sleeping* by Julie Markes
- *Good Enough to Eat* by Lizzy Rockwell (advanced)
- *Green Eggs and Ham* by Dr. Seuss
- *Olivia Cooks Up a Surprise* by Emily Sollinger

Activities:

- Practice flossing using an egg carton turned upside down. Pack play dough in between each raised section and then floss with yarn.
- Give your toys a bath.
- Have fun practicing hand washing with glitter, cocoa powder, or other "germs" at home.
- Make a healthy meal at home together.
- Exercise together.

Discussion:

- Discuss proper and polite ways to sneeze so that we don't spread germs.
- Talk about the importance of staying hydrated. Make a goal to drink a lot of water and fewer sugary drinks this week.
- It is also safe and healthy to wear sunscreen when outside. Discuss with your child why, how, and when sunscreen is used.
- Talk about healthy food options. Let her help you cook dinner.
- Reinforce the concept of eating large amounts of healthy foods and small amounts of unhealthy foods.

Unit 3: Things That Work
Lesson 15: Safety

Lesson Objective: Focus on ways to stay safe when exploring the many useful things around us. (This lesson serves as an introduction to all of Unit 3.)

Lesson 15 Skill Objectives:

- Attention span
- Critical thinking
- Following directions
- Gross motor
- Patience
- Safety awareness
- Social-emotional development
- Spatial awareness
- Taking turns
- Teamwork

Preparation

Lesson Materials:

- The following homemade signs mounted on cardstock and attached to a craft stick: stop sign, yield sign, walk sign (as seen at intersections)
- Pictures of fire, water, outlets, computers, chemicals, cars, guns, and roads
- Things to create obstacle course

Hands-on Activity Materials:

- Black, green, and red construction paper

Lesson 15 Outline

1. Welcome music/gather to carpets

2. Welcome song: "The More We Get Together"

3. Attention grabber: One, Two, Three, Now Follow Me!
   Skill: following directions

4. Calendar time
   Skills: patience, taking turns

5. Story time: *Play Safe!* by Margery Cuyler
   Skills: attention span, critical thinking

6. Transition activity: Stop, Drop, and Roll
   Skills: gross motor, safety awareness, spatial awareness

7. Lesson: Safety First
   Skills: critical thinking, gross motor, safety awareness, spatial awareness, teamwork, vocabulary

8. Hands-on activity: Red Light, Green Light
   Skills: following directions, gross motor

9. Theme song

10. Children dismissed for free play

Lesson 15 Details

Teacher Tip: Teach Safety

Use this lesson as an opportunity to emphasize, in a fun and interactive way, the importance of safety, obeying guidelines and rules, and being aware of dangers. Make sure you find the right balance of emphasizing safety without frightening the children. Make sure they know that staying safe helps us to feel happy!

Transition Activity: Stop, Drop, and Roll

Skills:

Explain that we use the "Stop, Drop, and Roll" movement if clothing ever catches on fire. (Emphasize we do not use this movement if we burn a finger or hear a fire alarm.) Demonstrate it, and have the children practice.

Lesson: Safety First

Skills: critical thinking, gross motor, right/left orientation, safety awareness, spatial awareness, teamwork, vocabulary

1. Explain the purpose of stop signs
    a. Hold up the **homemade stop sign**, and ask the children, "Do you know what this is?" Integrate a simple discussion of its color, shape, and letters.
    b. Talk about what a stop sign means. "What should we do when we see a stop sign? Do stop signs help keep us safe? Stop signs and red lights tell us when we need to stop so we don't get hurt."

2. Discuss the yield sign
    a. Hold up the **homemade yield sign** and discuss what it looks like, how many sides it has, what shape it is, what color it is, etc.
    b. Introduce the word *yield and talk about the difference between a stop sign and a yield sign: "A stop sign warns us that we should stop right away. A yield sign says we need to pause and be cautious before moving forward.
    c. Explain that stop and yield signs are there for our protection. They give us important messages about how to stay safe. Whether we are inside or outside, there are so many fascinating and important things that work. As we learn about these things, we must know when to stop and when to yield, so we can stay safe!

3. Discuss the walk sign

a. Hold up the **homemade walk sign** and talk about how this sign tells us when it is safe to cross the road. The walk sign is much like a green light.

4. Stop, yield and go!
    a. Explain that we are going to talk about several things that we might see in our houses, outside of our houses, or at someone else's house. These things are good things that can work to help us, but they can sometimes be dangerous. When we see these things we need to:
        i. Stop. Stop and freeze in place! (Hold up the stop sign, and have the children practice freezing with you.)
        ii. Yield. We think about what we need to do to make sure we are safe. (Hold up the yield sign.)
        iii. Go. We can go when we have done the right thing. (Hold up the walk sign.)
    b. Review the "stop, yield, and go" method with each of the following potential dangers before moving onto the Stop, Yield, and Go Game (step 13). Use the **photos or cutouts of fire, water, outlets, computers, chemicals, cars, guns, and roads** as you teach.

5. Fire
    a. Stop: Do not go near it! Do not run if it is on you!
    b. Yield: What do you need to do? If you see a fire, get as far away as possible, and find an adult. If your clothes catch on fire, you should stop, drop, and roll.
    c. Go: Are you safe? Good job!

6. Water
    a. Stop: If you see a swimming pool, lake, or any kind of water, stop!
    b. Yield: What do you need to do? Make sure an adult is with you and says it's ok to swim.
    c. Go: Is an adult with you? Yes! Have fun swimming!

7. Outlets
    a. Stop: When you see an outlet, don't touch it! Outlets contain *electricity*, which gives things in our house power to work. However, if we use outlets wrong, they can shock us, which could hurt!
    b. Yield: What do you need to do? Ask an adult for help if you need something plugged in or unplugged.
    c. Go: Good job! You asked for help!

8. Computers

a. Stop: Should we use a computer by ourselves? Computers have many wonderful games, programs, and movies, but they also have pictures and programs that can hurt our brains. We should never use computers by ourselves!

b. Yield: What do you need to do? Ask an adult for help. Follow your family's rules.

c. Go: Good job! You asked for help! Enjoy playing on the computer!

9. Chemicals/cleaners
   a. Stop: When you see a cleaner, don't touch, spray or drink it. Cleaners are for keeping our home clean, but they can be dangerous to children.
   b. Yield: What do you need to do? Tell an adult so it can be put away in a safe place.
   c. Go: Did you tell an adult? Good job! You kept yourself and others safe!

10. Cars
    a. Stop: Cars can get us from place to place, but they move very quickly, and we have to make sure we keep ourselves safe.
    b. Yield: What do you need to do? Before the car moves, we need to buckle our seat belts. (If you have a buckle, have the children take turns buckling it.)
    c. Go: Good job! Your seat belt is buckled, and you are ready to go for a ride!

11. Guns
    a. Stop: Guns are for adults only! They can be very dangerous to children.
    b. Yield: What do you need to do? If you see a gun, walk away and do not touch it. Then go tell an adult.
    c. Go: Did you walk away and tell an adult? Good job! You kept yourself and others safe!

12. Road
    a. Stop: Roads are places where cars, trucks, and other vehicles drive. It is important to cross safely when we are going on walks and riding our bikes.
    b. Yield: What do you need to do? Never go on a road unless you are holding an adult's hand! Always look right (practice!) and left (practice!) before crossing the street.
    c. Go: Did you hold someone's hand? Did you look both ways? Good for you! You can cross the street safely!

13. Stop, Yield, and Go Game
    a. Set up a **simple obstacle course** throughout the room. Start by asking one of the children to stand on the opposite side of the room. Have the other children take turns holding the stop, yield, and go signs.
    b. Tell the child doing the obstacle course that his goal is to make it safely across the room to give you a high five. (You can also use another incentive.) Tell him that

he will encounter an *obstacle* along the way and will need to remember to stop, yield, and go.

c. As the child starts across the room, place a cutout by one of the obstacles.
d. When the child reaches the obstacle, create a scenario related to the cutout for him to consider. (Ex: He is in a friend's backyard, which has a large pool.) Have the child with the stop sign hold up the stop sign up while everyone says "Stop!" together. Encourage the child in the scenario to freeze in place.
e. Have the child with the yield sign hold up the yield sign. Have that child ask, "What should you do?"
f. Once the child doing the obstacle course has answered the question correctly, the child with the walk sign holds up his sign, and the child who answered the question is free to proceed to the end of the course. High fives all around!
g. Repeat the game until everyone has had a turn, for as many times as the children's attention span will allow. Encourage participation by having different children hold the signs and involving everyone in the decision-making process during the "yield" phase of the game.
h. Optional: You may want to slightly change the obstacle course each time you choose a new child.

Hands-on Activity: Red Light, Green Light

Skills: following directions, gross motor

Before the activity, make a stoplight from **black, green, and red construction paper**. Start by gluing a red circle and a green circle to a whole piece of black construction paper (red on the top half, green on the bottom half, just like a traffic light). Cut another piece of black construction paper in half. Tape the top of the half piece of paper so it completely covers the bottom half of the whole piece of construction paper. (The tape should run right along the middle of the whole piece of construction paper.) When the light is green, flip up the half piece of black paper to cover the red circle and expose the green. To turn the light red, flip down the half piece of black paper to cover the green and expose the red.

Find a large area to play the game. (If weather allows, go outside.) Take several steps back from the children and explain that they should run to you when they see the green light and stop when they see the red. After a few rounds, take some time to talk about how we see stoplights on the road. They help to keep us safe because everyone knows how to obey the rules.

Lesson 15 Outing and Parental Supplement

Outing: Fire Station

Skills: social-emotional development, safety awareness

Arrange a tour of a fire station. (Let the station know beforehand that this week's lesson was about safety in general, so they can adapt their presentation as needed.) Firefighters deal with much more than just putting out fires, so visiting a fire station is a great chance to learn about other safety topics.

Parental Supplement

Books:

- *The Berenstain Bears Safe and Sound* by Jan and Mike Berenstain
- *Please Play Safe!* by Margery Cuyler
- *No Dragons for Tea* by Jean E. Pendziwol
- *A Treasure at Sea for Dragon and Me* by Jean E. Pendziwol
- *Officer Buckle and Gloria* by Peggy Rathmann

Activities:

- Play "flame" freeze tag! Cut out paper in the shape of flames, and put tape on them. Play a game of freeze tag where you stick a flame to the person you are chasing. Instead of freezing, they have to stop, drop, and roll.
- Go on a safety scavenger hunt around your neighborhood. (You can go in the car if it's too cold for a walk.) Have your child mark off the different kinds of signs and stoplights he sees. You could also make a bingo board.
- Take an inventory of your home together. Discuss different things found in your home and whether they are safe or not.
- Make your own stop signs and stick them on different objects around your home so your child knows what he should stay away from. (Optional: Some stores sell stickers that warn children not to drink or touch certain chemicals in your home. You could buy these, discuss their meaning, and place them together on the things your child should stay away from.)

Discussion:

Note: There are several safety issues that are extremely important to go over with your child but should be done on a one-on-one basis, at the discretion of the parent, and catered to your individual child's needs. Consider discussing the following with your child, based on the rules and guidelines you have established in your family. Make sure not to make this week's discussion frightening or heavy. Talk about how staying safe helps us to feel happy!

- Your family's policy on speaking to strangers; keeping children safe from potential kidnappings, abuse, getting lost, etc.; and what to do in case something ever does happen. This could include policies for when children are allowed to leave with another adult, family passwords, and any other safety procedures and rules your family has chosen to implement.
- Protecting children from sexual abuse by discussing appropriate vs. inappropriate touch; how and when to call 911; and rules for sharing personal information, such as name, phone number, and address.
- Your family's computer usage policy and what to do if your child encounters dangerous and/or pornographic material. (Ex: Crash then tell!)
- Any other safety plans your family has put into place regarding fire safety, water safety, road safety, etc.

Unit 3: Things That Work
Lesson 16: Things That Work around the House

Lesson Objective: Learn more about things that work around the house.

Lesson 16 Skill Objectives:

- Attention span
- Critical thinking
- Curiosity
- Following directions
- Gross motor
- Imaginative play
- Memory
- Patience
- Safety awareness
- Sensory development
- Social-emotional development
- Taking turns
- Visual tracking

Preparation

Lesson Materials:

- Lesson 16 Images
- Bowl
- Clean dish
- Small, wet towel
- Two small, dry towels
- Marshmallow
- Plate
- Toilet paper
- Dirty dish

Hands-on Activity Materials:

- Several copies of Lesson 16 Images
- Glue
- Construction paper
- Scissors

Lesson 16 Outline

1. Welcome music/gather to carpets

2. Welcome song: "The More We Get Together"

3. Attention grabber: Hocus Pocus, Everybody Focus!
   Skill: following directions

4. Calendar time
   Skills: patience, taking turns

5. Story time: *How Things Work in the House* by Lisa Campbell Ernst
   Skill: attention span

6. Transition activity: Toaster Poppers
   Skills: gross motor, imaginative play

7. Lesson: Things That Work around the House
   Skills: following directions, imaginative play, patience, safety awareness, sensory development

8. Hands-on activity: Memory
   Skills: critical thinking, fine motor, memory

9. Theme song

10. Children dismissed for free play

Lesson 16 Details

Teacher Tip: End Early as Needed

Remember to focus on the children's experience, not the amount of material covered or the length of the lessons. Some lessons may hold the children's interest for the entirety of the allotted time, while others may end more quickly. Do your best to provide an environment where learning is exciting and fun, but understand that lessons that end early provide more time for free play, which experts agree is among the most essential experiences for preschoolers!

Transition Activity: Toaster Poppers

Skills: gross motor, imaginative play

Briefly explain how a toaster works as the children act out what you're saying. (Ex: "Push down! It's getting hotter and hotter, and . . . pop!") At the end of your explanation, have them jump (or "pop") into the air.

Lesson: Things That Work around the House

Skills: following directions, imaginative play, safety awareness, sensory development, patience

1. Before the lesson, prepare your **Lesson 16 Images** according to the instructions in the hands-on activity. Place the images in a **bowl**. Also place a **clean dish** in the dishwasher, a **small, wet towel** in the washing machine, and a **small, dry towel** in the dryer.

2. To begin, explain that you will be taking the children on a tour of things that work around the house. Establish some rules for the tour (ex: stay with the group, don't touch things unless instructed to, etc).

3. Have a child pick one of the Lesson 16 Images from the bowl. Make sure all the children see the picture and know what it is, so they will recognize these pictures for the hands-on activity later.

4. Go to that item. Ask the children to tell you what they already know about that item, then teach them more about what that item does. Discuss how adults properly and safely use the item. Finish by demonstrating how to use the item. (Demonstrations explained below.)

5. At the end of your demonstration, have another child pick another picture from the bowl. Continue until you have discussed all of the things that work around the house.

6. Demonstrations
    a. Microwave: Place a **marshmallow** on a **plate** and place the plate in the microwave. Cook for less than 1 minute. You may need to do this demo a few times so that each child has a chance to watch. (Test the timing beforehand so you can cook the marshmallow long enough to puff up but not so long that it explodes.)
    b. Toilet: Allow the children to take turns flushing a small amount of **toilet paper**.
    c. Oven: For safety reasons, you won't really be using the oven. Explain how it works and how to stay safe while using it. (Optional: Prepare a pretend demo of something baking.)
    d. Light bulb: Find a room that has a light switch and that will have a noticeable difference in light when the switch is turned on and off. Allow each child to have a turn with the switch.
    e. Faucet: Show that faucets open to allow water to flow and close to stop the water. You can also have the children touch the water and feel for different temperatures. (Safety note: Make sure the water isn't too hot so the children don't burn themselves.)
    f. Dishwasher: Before the lesson, place one clean dish in the dishwasher. During the lesson, show the children a similar looking **dirty dish**, and place it inside. Pretend that the dishwasher runs a cycle, and pull out the clean dish.
    g. Laundry Machine: Before the lesson, place one small wet towel in the washing machine and a similar looking dry towel in the dryer. During the lesson (with the children watching), place **a second small, dry towel** in the washer and pretend that the washing machine runs a cycle. Have the children imagine what's going on inside the machine. First the washer fills up with water, so have them hold their breath like they are in water. Next it swishes the clothes all around, so have the children wiggle and twist. Then the washer lets all the water out and spins really fast, so have the children spin. (Make sure the children have enough space to move around without getting hurt.) Pull out the wet towel (the one previously placed there) and put it in the dryer. Pretend to let the dryer run one cycle. Pull out the dry towel (which was previously placed there).
    h. Air conditioning/heater: Show the children the thermostat and change the temperature so that the machine switches on or off. Explain how the air coming out is either warm or cold (depending on what you set it to) in order to keep us comfortable in our homes.

Hands-on Activity: Memory

Skills: critical thinking, fine motor, memory

Before the lesson, **make several copies of the Lesson 16 Images** (one set for you and one set for each child). **Glue construction paper** to the back of your set (so the children can't see through the paper) and cut out the squares with **scissors**. Play Memory with the children, letting them turn over the squares two at a time until they make a match. Send each child home with a copy of the Lesson 16 Images so she can play with her family. (She can cut the squares out at home with her parents, or you can do it before class.)

Lesson 16 Outing and Parental Supplement

Outing: Hardware Store

Skills: curiosity, gross motor, social-emotional development, sensory development

Visit your nearest hardware store (ex: Home Depot, Lowe's, Ace Hardware). Let the children safely explore the store. Talk about all the things they see. Visit the section with appliances, and let the children see some of the household items they learned about in the lesson. Ask an employee to explain how something works. Optional: Use the printouts from Lesson 16 Images to have a scavenger hunt.

Parental Supplement

Books:

- *The Pink Refrigerator* by Tim Egan
- *How Things Work in the House* by Lisa Campbell Ernst
- *How Things Work* by Conrad Mason
- *How Our House Works* by Ed Strauss
- *If I Built a House* by Chris Van Dusen

Activities:

- Play the memory game that the children made during lesson time.
- Sometimes things that do work around the house break. Explain that we can fix them ourselves or call someone to repair them for us. Pretend to be a repair person and fix things around the house. Talk about what it would be like if you didn't have those things (no light bulbs, no faucet, etc.).
- Allow your child to help with chores. Which items (and people) work around the house?
- Cook together, or do any household task that requires items discussed in the lesson.
- Visit a store that specializes in repairs (ex: clock repairs, piano repairs, or appliance repairs). Ask if your child can observe someone at work, and enjoy an inside look at how things work.

Discussion:

- Talk about how we use tools to keep things in our home working.
- Discuss which items around the house your child is allowed to operate alone and which ones require supervision.
- Discuss items that are off-limits. Review the safety rules discussed in Lesson 15.

Resources Used by Authors:
- www.clker.com

Unit 3: Things That Work
Lesson 17: Things That Work outside the House

Lesson Objective: Learn more about things that work outside the house in a fun and interactive way while strengthening cognition with simple mental exercises.

Lesson 17 Skill Objectives:

- Attention span
- Creativity
- Critical thinking
- Curiosity
- Expressive language
- Fine motor
- Following directions
- Gross motor
- Imaginative play
- Memory

- Music appreciation
- Patience
- Perspective
- Problem solving
- Resourcefulness
- Social-emotional development
- Sensory development
- Taking turns
- Teamwork

Preparation

Transition Activity Materials:

- LMG SUGGESTED SONG LIST

Lesson Materials:

- *Building a Road* by Henry Pluckrose*
- Several household objects that can be used to mimic road-building tools**

*This lesson requires pictures of vehicles that do roadwork. If you cannot find this book, ask your librarian for suggestions, or print several pictures from the internet.

**Some items can be obvious solutions (ex: a spoon represents an excavator, or a rolling pin makes a great road roller). In addition to some obvious items, however, make sure that you gather plenty of abstract items so you can see what the children come up with on their own.

Hands-on Activity Materials:

- Toothpicks
- Large marshmallows
- Blocks (optional)

Lesson 17 Outline

1. Welcome music/gather to carpets

2. Welcome song: "The More We Get Together"

3. Attention grabber: Do What I'm Doing
   Skill: following directions

4. Calendar time
   Skills: patience, taking turns

5. Story time: *Goodnight, Goodnight, Construction Site* by Sherri Duskey Rinker
   Skill: attention span

6. Transition activity: "London Bridge"
   Skills: gross motor, music appreciation

7. Lesson: Building, Fixing, Working
   Skills: creativity, expressive language, gross motor, imaginative play, memory, perspective, resourcefulness, teamwork

8. Hands-on activity: Marshmallow Construction
   Skills: creativity, fine motor, imaginative play, problem solving

9. Theme song

10. Children dismissed for free play

Lesson 17 Details

Teacher Tip: Challenge Your Students

This lesson incorporates a lot of memory, imagination, and teamwork—it is designed to stretch both the children and the teacher! As you push the children to develop and explore new skills, adapt the lesson to their abilities and attention spans. If you can tell that a certain part of this activity will be beyond their current cognitive abilities, simplify as needed. Feel free to skip some parts and embellish others. Help the children have fun while challenging their minds within their capacities.

Transition Activity: "London Bridge"

Skills: gross motor, music appreciation

Sing "London Bridge" (#15 on the **LMG SUGGESTED SONG LIST**; see Appendix C for lyrics). Have two children stand facing each other, hands clasped together over their heads. The other children walk under their arms until the last line of the song ("my fair lady"), at which point their arms come down, trapping whomever is between them. Have fun and get wiggles out!

Optional: Sing as many verses of this song as you'd like. You can sing only the first verse so the children can focus more on the game, or you can add verses and either continue with the game, or do pantomimes together to fit the different verses of the song.

Lesson: Building, Fixing, Working

Skills: creativity, expressive language, gross motor, imaginative play, memory, perspective, resourcefulness, teamwork

1. Page through *Building a Road* by Henry Pluckrose to refresh the children's memory of some of the objects and vehicles they learned about during story time. (If the book is not available, show them pictures of vehicles and tools used in roadwork.)

2. Have them describe roadwork vehicles:
    a. Show them one large photograph (like a bulldozer). Let them look closely at the picture. Tell them you are going to close the book and have them describe it.
    b. Close the book and ask one child to describe what a bulldozer looks like. He may need some prompting, but let him do as much as he can on his own! Even if he doesn't know how to do this activity at first, give him plenty of chances to try. This is an exercise that will challenge his memory, his ability to process and verbalize information, and his vocabulary, all of which aid in his cognitive

development. Optional: Have all the children try and describe the roadwork vehicle together.

    c. After the child has described the vehicle, ask him to look through the pile of **household objects** and see if he can find something to "be" a bulldozer. (This can be as simple as finding something that he can use to push other objects out of the way.)

    d. Repeat several times until each child is assigned a different vehicle or tool used in roadwork.

3. Explain that we will work together to pretend to build a road, just like in the books we have just read. Everyone will have a different part, and it is important to work together as a team to get the job done.

4. There are several different ways that you can pretend to build a road together. Use one of these options, or come up with one on your own:

    a. Build a road in a sandbox with your tools. For example, dig the sand with your "excavator," push the sand out of the way with the "bulldozer," pretend to pour tar or cement with the "cement mixer or grader," and use your "road roller" to smooth it out. You can use other tools or machines as well—there are many possibilities!

    b. Build a road using any other medium you have, such as play dough or a sensory bin.

    c. Use your imaginations and simply use the tools to pretend you are doing all of these actions on the floor.

    d. Note: Understand that some parallel play is to be expected in this activity. If the children are all occupied with their own task and ignoring each other, that is normal. When appropriate, encourage them to work together to build the road.

Hands-on Activity: Marshmallow Construction

Skills: creativity, fine motor, imaginative play, problem solving

Have the children construct their own buildings using **toothpicks** and **large marshmallows**. When buildings inevitably topple, talk about how fixing is an important part of building. Ask what types of tools people use to fix structural problems when building. Pretend to use hammers, nails, and other types of tools. Encourage the children to come up with solutions to their problems first, helping only as needed. As they build, ask them about the type of buildings they are making and who will use their building. Allow their imaginations to work as they build. Above all, eat lots of marshmallows and have fun! Optional: For a much simpler activity, build with **blocks**.

Lesson 17 Outing and Parental Supplement

Outing: Construction Site

Skills: curiosity, social-emotional development, sensory development

Based on your weather conditions and local availability, pick one of the following options: watch snow plows, observe a construction site from a safe distance, visit a local recycling center, or find a children's museum or science center where the children can practice building things.

Parental Supplement

Books:

- *Road Builders* by B.G. Hennessy
- *Machines Go to Work in the City* by William Low
- *Building a Road* by Henry Pluckrose
- *Goodnight, Goodnight, Construction Site* by Sherri Duskey Rinker
- *Roadwork Ahead* by Anastasia Suen
- *Construction* by Sally Sutton
- *Demolition* by Sally Sutton
- *Road Work* by Sally Sutton

Activities:

- Work together with play dough. Talk about the different things you can build together. Ask your child to tell you about what he is building.
- If there is construction going on in your area, go watch! Talk about the different machines, vehicles, and tools. Talk about how they work together, and talk about what they are accomplishing.
- Build with blocks or any other toy that your child loves. Let him build whatever he likes. Ask him to tell you about it.
- Play, dig, or build in the dirt or sand. Use toy trucks, shovels, buckets, sticks, leaves, etc. Pretend to be some of the machines. For a fun twist, add some water.
- Build and dig in play dough, dirt, or sand using different household objects, like spoons, rolling pins, plastic knives, or straws.
- If you visited the recycling plant for the outing this week, practice resourcefulness and look for some garbage that you can make something new from.
- Build gingerbread houses with graham crackers and frosting.
- Build roads together out of meat and cheese at lunchtime.

Discussion:

- When something breaks, talk together about how you would fix it. Before offering solutions of your own, ask your child what he would like to do. Help him learn to problem solve.
- As you drive in the car, ask what kinds of things he sees. Point out the things you see that work. Talk about how they work and why they work. Ask a lot of questions, and answer them together.
- Ask your child which construction vehicle is his favorite and why.

Resources Used by Authors:
- http://www.rhymes.org.uk/london-bridge-is-falling-down.htm

# Unit 3: Things That Work
Lesson 18: Music and Instruments

Lesson Objective: Learn about different types of musical instruments and how they work, while practicing rhythms and gaining new exposure to music.

Lesson 18 Skill Objectives:

- Attention span
- Curiosity
- Emotional awareness
- Expressive language
- Fine motor
- Following directions
- Gross motor
- Imaginative play
- Individuality
- Leadership
- Listening
- Music appreciation
- Patience
- Pre-math
- Rhythm
- Sensory development
- Social-emotional development
- Taking turns
- Teamwork
- Vocabulary

Preparation

Transition Activity Materials:
- LMG SUGGESTED SONG LIST

Lesson Materials:
- Egg shaker: plastic eggs, beans, tape
- Straw pipes: scissors, cardboard or heavy paper, glue, 6 straws
- Rubber band guitar: six rubber bands, empty tissue box
- Picture of symphony orchestra
- Recording of orchestra playing (we suggest *Peter and the Wolf* by Prokofiev, or the *1812 Overture* or *The Sleeping Beauty* (the ballet) by Tchaikovsky

Hands-on Activity Materials:
- LMG SUGGESTED SONG LIST
- Other songs children will enjoy dancing to (optional)

Lesson 18 Outline

1. Welcome music/gather to carpets

2. Welcome song: "The More We Get Together"

3. Attention grabber: Stand Up! Sit Down.
   Skills: following directions, gross motor

4. Calendar time
   Skills: patience, taking turns

5. Story time: *Zin! Zin! Zin! A Violin* by Lloyd Moss
   Skills: attention span, pre-math, vocabulary

6. Transition activity: "The Orchestra"
   Skills: imaginative play, music appreciation

7. Lesson: Our Orchestra
   Skills: attention span, emotional awareness, expressive language, fine motor, following directions, gross motor, leadership, music appreciation, rhythm, teamwork, vocabulary

8. Hands-on activity: Dancing
   Skills: gross motor, individuality, music appreciation, rhythm

9. Theme song

10. Children dismissed for free play

Lesson 18 Details

Teacher Tip: Play Music

Music helps children's brains grow and make connections in ways that no other activity can accomplish. For example, as we sing, we emphasize the pronunciation of words, which can increase a child's language development. The patterns children find in music furthermore help their brains prepare for reading and increase their memory. The activities in this lesson will also help with rhythm, pitch, creativity, self-expression, and gross motor development. Music can bring great joy to our lives and create fun moments for children, teachers, and families!

Transition Activity: "The Orchestra"

Skills: imaginative play, music appreciation

Explain what an orchestra is and how it works. (Ex: "A lot of people work as a team to play their instruments together. They have to listen to each other, follow the music, and follow the conductor. Each person is important!") Play "The Orchestra" (#16 on the **LMG SUGGESTED SONG LIST**). Pretend to play the instruments and make their sounds, or simply sing along with the instruments. The words/sounds are as follows:

> Violin: va vaa... va vaa…
> Clarinet: doodle-doodle-doodle-doodle-det
> Trumpet: tat-tat-tat-tat…
> Trombone: doo-ah…
> Drum: boom boom boom boom...

Lesson: Our Orchestra

Skills: attention span, emotional awareness, expressive language, fine motor, following directions, gross motor, leadership, music appreciation, rhythm, teamwork, vocabulary

1. Make the following instruments prior to the lesson:
    a. Egg shaker: Fill **plastic eggs** with **beans** and **tape** securely closed. Make enough for each child to take one home. Optional: Make the egg shakers together. Safety note: Make sure younger siblings stay away from the many choking hazards.
    b. Straw pipes: Use **scissors** to cut the **cardboard or heavy paper** into two rectangles (about 2 inches by 6 inches). Place one rectangle flat and horizontal. **Glue** the **6 straws** perpendicular, evenly spaced, with about an inch sticking above the top of the paper. Glue the other rectangle on top so the straws are sandwiched. Cut the bottom of the straws at different lengths so they are tiered. Make enough for each child to take one home.

c. Rubber band guitar: Wrap the **6 rubber bands** around the **empty tissue box**. (Use slightly different sizes and widths of rubber bands to get different sounds.) Make enough for each child to take one home.

2. Begin by teaching the children more about a symphony orchestra and how it works.
    a. Hold up a **picture of a symphony orchestra**, preferably one that clearly shows the conductor and several different instruments being played. Ask the children if they recognize any of the instruments. Point out that some of the instruments are **percussion* instruments, some are wind instruments, and some are string instruments.
    b. Optional: Mention that some symphony orchestras also have a brass section, which includes trumpets, trombones, French horns, etc. We will not be using brass instruments in our orchestra for this lesson.

3. Play a **recording of an orchestra performing**. (Some of our favorites are *Peter and the Wolf* by Prokofiev, or the *1812 Overture* or *The Sleeping Beauty* (the ballet) by Tchaikovsky. These pieces have wonderful melodies and tell great stories, making them ideal pieces to listen to with children.)
    a. Ask, "What are the different sounds you can hear? Can you tell the difference between all of the sounds?" Discuss the concept of everyone working as a team to make a more beautiful sound together than any of them could make on their own. Ask the children how the music makes them feel or what kind of story the musicians are telling through their music. Ask, "Does this music sound happy? Sad? Scary? Peaceful?" Encourage them to use their own words to describe how the music makes them feel.
    b. Optional: Briefly explain the role of the **conductor*. Practice conducting together as you listen to the music.

4. Teach the children about three of the main types of musical instruments: percussion, winds, and strings. For each type, briefly explain how the instruments work, pass out the corresponding homemade instrument, and play "Keep the Beat" by showing the class how to play the instruments in a steady beat of four counts. Once they have mastered that, try a different simple rhythm. Have them copy you.
    a. Percussion (egg shakers): A percussion instrument works when we hit or tap it with our hand or a stick. There are lots of types of percussion instruments, like drums, cymbals, triangles, and tambourines.
    b. Winds (straw pipes): A wind instrument works when we blow air through it, causing vibrations that make sounds. The sound changes depending on how long or short the instrument is and how fast we blow the air. There are a lot of types of wind instruments, like pipes, harmonicas, flutes, and clarinets.
    c. Strings (rubber band guitar): A string instrument works when strings are played and then **vibrate* to make sound. The sound also **echoes* inside the instrument.

There are a lot of types of string instruments, like the violin, viola, guitar, cello, and harp.

5. Create a class orchestra by having each child play a different instrument. Talk about the importance of each member as you listen to each other and make music together. You could pretend to be the conductor and ask the children to watch and follow you as you lead the music. Allow them to take turns conducting as well. Optional: Turn on orchestral music and have the children play along or take turns conducting.

Hands-on Activity: Dancing

Skills: gross motor, individuality, music appreciation, rhythm

Have the children dance along to songs from the **LMG SUGGESTED SONG LIST** or **other songs** you think they might like. Choose songs with varying sounds, tempos, and rhythms. Have fun dancing together and celebrate each child's individual movement!

Lesson 18 Outing and Parental Supplement

Outing: Music Store

Skills: curiosity, listening, music appreciation, rhythm, social-emotional development, sensory development

Visit a local music store. If none are available in your area, hold a parade with the children instead. They can play their homemade instruments in the marching band and use their bikes or other toys as floats. (Use a local gymnasium if weather doesn't permit an outdoor parade.)

Parental Supplement

Books:

- *Violet's Music* by Angela Johnson
- *Can You Hear It?* by William Lach
- *Just a Little Music* by Mercer Mayer
- *Zin! Zin! Zin! A Violin* by Lloyd Moss
- *M is for Melody: A Music Alphabet* by Kathy-jo Wargin

Activities:

- Make some homemade instruments (water glasses, castanets, maracas, etc.) and create music together. Review how each instrument works.
- Practice rhythms with clapping, stomping, etc. Have your child copy the rhythms you make
- Practice pitch. Sing a note and vowel sound (like "Ah") and see if your child can match it. Change the pitch and vowel (like "Oh"). Try again. Repeat.
- If you didn't do this for the group outing, have a family parade.
- Listen to all kinds of music together as a family. Talk about how different music makes you feel. Consider listening to some of the orchestral pieces suggested in this lesson.
- Listen to different types of music throughout the day that are appropriate for different situations. (Ex: listen to upbeat music while you clean up or do chores, and listen to calming music while getting ready for bed.)
- Have a dance party.
- As a family, attend a concert where you can view several different types of instruments. Talk about the role of a conductor and the concept of working together as a team to make beautiful music.
- Listen to or watch recordings from the three orchestral pieces listed in the lesson.

Discussion:

- Do you have any musical instruments in your home? Do any family members play instruments?

- What are some of our favorite songs to sing? Practice them!
- Where are some places where we hear music (home, store, concert, church)?
- Talk about what music lessons, if any, your child may like to take in the future.

Resources Used by Authors:
- http://www.musicologyaz.com
- http://en.wikipedia.org

Unit 3: Things That Work
Lesson 19: You Work—I Can Help at Home

Lesson Objective: Give children a sense of responsibility and importance as they learn that working hard and helping others can be fun and empowering.

Lesson 19 Skill Objectives:

- Attention span
- Creativity
- Fine motor
- Following directions
- Gross motor
- Imaginative play
- Patience
- Responsibility
- Rhyming
- Self-esteem
- Taking turns

Preparation

Lesson Materials:

- None

Hands-on Activity Materials:

- Lesson 19 Images: Superkid logo (one for each child)
- Cape for each child*
- Glitter, puff paints, markers, crayons (optional)
- Cardstock (optional)
- Safety pins

*You can provide the capes yourself or ask the parents to do so. Some options include a towel (tie around the neck or attach a simple clasp), an adult T-shirt (cut away the arms and the front of the shirt, leaving the back of the T-shirt as a cape and the neckline intact to go around the child's neck), or fabric (cut and sew into a cape a simple clasp or fastener at the neck).

Lesson 19 Outline

1. Welcome music/gather to carpets

2. Welcome song: "The More We Get Together"

3. Attention grabber: Hands on Top, That Means Stop!
   Skill: following directions

4. Calendar time
   Skills: patience, taking turns

5. Story time: *The Little Red Hen* by Diane Muldrow
   Skill: attention span

6. Transition activity: Superhero Stance and Run
   Skills: following directions, gross motor, imaginative play

7. Hands-on activity: Superhero Capes*
   Skills: creativity, fine motor gross motor, responsibility, rhyming, self-esteem

8. Lesson: Superkid to the Rescue Hands-on activity: Superhero Capes
   Skills: gross motor, responsibility, rhyming, self-esteem

9. Theme song

10. Children dismissed for free play

*Note that the order of the hands-on activity and lesson are switched for today only

Lesson 19 Details

Teacher Tip: Get Wiggles Out

Allowing children to move or "get their wiggles out" helps them focus on subsequent tasks and instructions. During this lesson, don't rush through the poem. Give the necessary time for the children to move around, play, pretend, and interact with each other. It may seem wild for a minute, but this activity fulfills an important developmental need for them, and you will notice their ability to focus increases after those fun moments.

Transition Activity: Superhero Stance and Run

Skills: following directions, gross motor, imaginative play

Explain to the children that they will become superheroes in today's lesson! They will become a superhero named Superkid with the magical power to help their families at home. Before beginning the lesson and activity, they must practice standing and running like a superhero. Teach them to stand like Superman with their feet apart, one hand on their hip, and the other arm extended out in front of them with that hand in a fist. Have them run around the room saying, "Superkid to the rescue!"

Hands-on Activity: Superhero Capes

Skills: creativity, fine motor

Let the children decorate their Superkid logos (**Lesson 19 Images**) and **capes** using **glitter, puff paints, markers, or crayons**. (If desired, print the Superkid logos on **cardstock** so they're stiffer.) Fasten the logo onto the cape with **safety pins**. As they decorate, talk about how they are preparing to be superheroes when they go home. Encourage them to wear their capes when they help around the house. Optional: Make simple masks for the superheroes.

Lesson: Superkid to the Rescue

Skills: gross motor, responsibility, rhyming, self-esteem

6. With the children wearing their capes, act out the following poem together as you read it aloud. This can be done in many effective ways. Try changing roles, taking turns, performing as a group, etc.

7. Feel free to substitute "mother" with father, aunt, grandmother, or whoever the child's primary caregiver is. You can also substitute "Superkid" with the child's name (ex: "Super Eli").

8. Anytime Superkid does something superhero-like, encourage the children to do their superhero stance and run! Use any of the suggested pantomimes below, and make up plenty of your own. Encourage a lot of movement and actions throughout the acting portion.

   Superkid!
   (A poem about being helpful)

   There once was a mother
   So busy and tired.
   She worked day and night
   With no chance to retire!

   She had many chores
   That kept her so busy.
   She said, "Oh, these messes
   Are making me dizzy!

   If only I had
   Someone come to my aid,
   But who could that be?
   I wish for a maid!"

   And then, who walked in?
   Why, a guest in disguise!
   "Who is it?" Mom said.
   "Oh, what a surprise!"

   This strange tiny person
   Spoke up right away:
   "The name's SUPERKID!
   And I've come here to stay! *(Superhero pose and run)*

   Don't worry, dear Mother,
   I'm so grown up now!
   I can help you as much
   As you will allow!

There are so many times
When I'll need your help still.
But as long as you're helping,
I promise I will.

I'll empty the dishwasher
If you take the knives out.
I can help you sort laundry,
Without any doubt.

I can dust off the bookshelves
If you show me how.
I'll sweep, mop, clean bathrooms,
And then take a bow! *(Bow)*

For Superkid is
That amazing, you see.
By the time I am done,
You'll be shouting with glee! *(Jump and shout "Hooray!")*

I might need your help
As I make my bed,
Set the table, make dinner,
Or help you make bread.

But then, there are things
I could do all alone.
I can pick up my toys!
I can answer the phone!

I can help with the babies
Who are younger than I!
I can help get you diapers
And not make them cry!

Don't you worry, dear Mother—
I know you work hard.
But with Superkid here, *(Superhero pose and run)*
You can take down your guard!

I know helping you,
Makes me happy, you see.

'Cause when I help out,
I feel good about me! *(Point both thumbs towards your chest)*

I'm here to show you
That you've raised me right.
I love you! I'll help you!
With all of my might!" *(Muscle pose)*

SUPERKID to the rescue! *(Say all together as they pose and run)*

Lesson 19 Outing and Parental Supplement

Outing: Service Scavenger Hunt

Skills: gross motor, responsibility, teamwork

1. Make a list of several very simple chores that the class can do together. The following are a few ideas to get you started:
    a. Dust a bookshelf.
    b. Sort laundry. (We suggest something simple like sorting socks into different piles by color. This teaches them the principle of helping and also aids their pre-math development through sorting.)
    c. Pick up toys.
    d. Help wash windows. (Children can use rags to wipe while the adults handle the chemicals—see Lesson 15.)
    e. Sweep a floor (each child taking a turn with the broom).

2. Make a list of places to go together. You can do something as simple as going to each of your own houses, or you can ask close friends or family members ahead of time if they'd be willing to participate. Plan ahead for this, since the person whom you are "serving" will need to agree beforehand—they might have more work after you are finished than before you started! (Ex: Windows may not be any cleaner after the children help out.)

3. Tell the children that "the mess monster" has attacked the houses on the list. Have the children put on their capes and run to the rescue.

4. Do as many chores at as many places as you would like. Allow children to physically check things off of the list when they are done.

5. Once your checklist is complete, gather to celebrate, praise their accomplishments, and discuss how helping others and working hard made them feel. Talk to them about how it feels good to relax and play after we've worked hard. If time allows, consider playing at the park or going out for ice cream together.

6. Alternative outing: clean up a park by picking up trash or pulling weeds.

Parental Supplement

Books:
- *The Berenstain Bears and the Trouble with Chores* by Stan and Jan Berenstain
- *Can I Help?* by Marilyn Janowitz

- *Helping Mom* by Mercer Mayer
- *Just Helping My Dad* by Mercer Mayer
- *The Little Red Hen* by Diane Muldrow

Activities:

- This week presents a great opportunity to introduce your child to simple chores and responsibilities in the home. Make a chore chart together, and let your child choose stickers to mark off each task. Decide together on incentives or rewards for filling up a day, week, or month of completed responsibilities.
- Read and act out the Superkid poem together at home while doing chores together. Encourage your child to wear his Superkid costume while picking up toys and performing other responsibilities.
- Consider using the following phrase for recruiting help with chores at home. Parent: "Who on earth can I find to save me from this awful mess [or whatever chore needs doing]?" Child: "Super [his name here] to the rescue!"
- Teach your child phone etiquette. Teach him polite ways to answer the phone and how to respond appropriately to callers.
- Play games together while working. Pretend to be superheroes and make toys "disappear" by cleaning them up, or turn cleaning into a chance to use up energy and run around the house together. Use timers or other incentives to see how fast you can get things done. Teach children that working together can be fun!

Discussion:

- Use positive reinforcement as you teach your child the importance of work. Praise him often, and encourage him by expressing your confidence in his abilities.
- Push him past his comfort levels in some areas by showing him that you believe he is capable. Believe that he can surprise you with what he is capable of and ready for.
- Point out every time your child does something helpful. Teach him the importance of saying thank you by setting an example.
- Talk to your child about how he feels inside when he helps other people. Teach him that working hard and helping others makes us happy.

Unit 3: Things That Work
Lesson 20: You Work—Occupations

Lesson Objective: Learn about several occupations and help the children imagine all of the amazing possibilities ahead of them.

Lesson 20 Skill Objectives:

- Accountability
- Attention span
- Creativity
- Critical thinking
- Curiosity
- Expressive language
- Fine motor
- Following directions
- Goal setting
- Gross motor

- Imaginative play
- Patience
- Pre-math
- Respect
- Self-esteem
- Social-emotional development
- Taking turns
- Teamwork
- Vocabulary

Preparation

Lesson Materials:

- Glue
- Lesson 20 Images pages 1–4 (one copy)
- Nine plastic cups
- Scissors

- Crayons
- Lesson 20 Images page 6 (enough for each child)
- Lesson 20 Images page 7 (one copy)

Hands-on Activity Materials:

- Yarn or string to make necklaces
- Tape

- Lesson 20 Images page 5, cut and hole-punched (enough for each child)

Parent Responsibility:

- Have child come with a costume or prop representing an occupation

Lesson 20 Outline

1. Welcome music/gather to carpets

2. Welcome song: "The More We Get Together"

3. Attention grabber: One, Two, Three, Now Follow Me!
   Skill: following directions

4. Calendar time
   Skills: patience, taking turns

5. Story time: *Busy Workers* by Richard Scarry
   Skill: attention span

6. Transition activity: Costume Runway
   Skills: expressive language, self-esteem

7. Lesson: Career Day
   Skills: creativity, critical thinking, fine motor, goal setting, pre-math, teamwork, vocabulary

8. Hands-on activity: Role Play
   Skills: imaginative play, leadership, taking turns, teamwork

9. Theme song

10. Children dismissed for free play

Lesson 20 Details

Teacher Tip: Encourage Language Development

Some important language goals for preschoolers include talking/dialogue, expressive/descriptive language, and articulating opinions and emotions. Use this lesson as a time to help the children develop these skills. For example, have them talk to each other about what they are dressed up as, and encourage them to describe their costume and props. When they are discussing what they want to be when they grow up, encourage them to explain why they might enjoy that job. You may notice that they all want to pick the same answer, so try to help them express honest opinions.

Transition Activity: Costume Runway

Skills: expressive language, self-esteem

Structure this activity like Show and Tell. Let each child have a turn to stand in front of the class, show what she is wearing or what prop she brought, and talk about the occupation it represents.

Lesson: Career Day

Skills: creativity, critical thinking, fine motor, goal setting, pre-math, teamwork, vocabulary

1. Before the lesson, **glue** one cutout of a career person (**Lesson 20 Images pages 1–4**) to the outside of each cup (**nine plastic cups** total). Use **scissors** to cut out the other pictures from Lesson 20 images (pages 1–4) and mix them all together. (The children will sort these later.)

2. Introduce the lesson by explaining that adults work for many reasons. They help the *community, do what they enjoy, earn money, and more. It can take a lot of time, hard work, and education to become what you've dreamed of becoming. When you grow up, you can be whatever you want to be. Let's learn about some things people do for work.

3. In your own words, briefly review the occupations listed below as you hold up the corresponding cup. As you review each occupation, ask, What does this person do? How does this job help others? What things does this person use in order to do his or her work? After each occupation, say (as a class), "I can be a(n) _____!"
    a. Firefighter
    b. Police officer
    c. Doctor

136

d. Teacher
   e. Chef
   f. Farmer
   g. Construction worker
   h. Garbage collector
   i. Astronaut

4. Line up the nine cups in front of the children. Put the pile of objects from Lesson 20 Images (pages 1–4) where all of the children can see. One at a time, explain what each item is, then see if the children can figure out which occupation would need that item. Place the corresponding items inside the cup.

5. Have the children complete a career questionnaire :
   a. Have the children use **crayons** to color the person at the bottom of **Lesson 20 Images page 6** and pick a hat (**Lesson 20 Images page 7**) that they want to paste on the person.
   b. While the children are coloring, go around and ask the questions on the paper (Lesson 20 Images page 6) and fill it in for them. For the bottom two questions, have children identify what their parents/relatives do for work. (See if the children can identify the occupations before you help them.) Send this page home so parents can read their cute answers!

Hands-on Activity: Necklace Craft and Role Play

Skills: imaginative play, leadership, taking turns, teamwork

Before the activity, cut pieces of **yarn or string** to a length appropriate for necklaces. Put a small piece of **tape** at both ends of each piece of yarn (to make it easier to string things on). During the activity, pass out the career badges (**Lesson 20 Images page 5, cut and hole-punched**). (Each child should receive every badge.) Pass out the yarn, and have the children string their badges to make a necklace. Help them tie their badge necklaces loosely around their necks.

Gather the children back to the mat area. Take turns having each child come to the front. Let her pick an occupation (it doesn't have to be one covered in the lesson). Help prompt her how to act out that occupation while the other children play along in supporting roles. For example, one child is the teacher, and the rest are the class; one child is a firefighter, and the rest are people who get saved by the firefighter; or one child is a chef, and the rest are the people eating at the restaurant.

Lesson 20 Outing and Parental Supplement

Outing: Workplaces

Skills: curiosity, respect, social-emotional development, vocabulary

Arrange to have a tour of any workplace and learn more about what people do there. Optional: Visit the place a child's parent works.

Parental Supplement

Books:

- *When I Grow Up* by P.K. Hallinan
- *Clothesline Clues to Jobs People Do* by Kathryn Heling and Deborah Hembrook
- *Mousetronaut* by Astronaut Mark Kelly
- *Big Frank's Fire Truck* by Leslie McGuire
- *Career Day* by Anne Rockwell
- *Busy, Busy Town* by Richard Scarry
- *Busy Workers* by Richard Scarry
- *What Do People Do All Day?* by Richard Scarry
- *When I Grow Up* by Al Yankovic

Activities:

- Ask if you can bring your child to visit a family (or friend's) place of work. See if the workplace has a "Bring Your Child to Work" day.
- Watch for when the garbage truck comes. Wave to the garbage collector, and watch him or her work.
- Visit some other local community helpers, like librarians, farmers, construction workers, etc. Ask them why they chose to do what they do and why they love it. Talk about the ways they serve our community.
- Write a thank you note to a community helper that has positively influenced your child's life. Pretend to be a mail carrier and deliver your note, or give it to your mail carrier for delivery.

Discussion:

- What things do Mommy and Daddy love about their work? What are some challenges they have?
- Review Lesson 19 and ask what work your child can do around your house or neighborhood to earn income, help the community, and enjoy her job (task).
- Ask your child what she wants to be when she grows up and why. Let her share her dreams with you.

Unit 4: Things That Move
Lesson 21: Occupational Vehicles

Lesson Objective: Match the occupation to the correct vehicle and location while having fun, moving, and practicing taking turns.

Lesson 21 Skill Objectives:

- Attention span
- Critical thinking
- Curiosity
- Expressive language
- Fine motor
- Following directions
- Gross motor
- Imaginative play
- Memory
- Music appreciation
- Patience
- Social-emotional development
- Taking turns
- Visualization

Preparation

Transition Activity Materials:

- LMG SUGGESTED SONG LIST

Lesson Materials:

- Tape
- Lesson 21 Images pages 2–8
- Props that represent the following occupations: fire fighter, police officer, doctor, farmer, construction worker, astronaut
- Round object or toy to represent steering wheel (like a plate)

Hands-on Activity Materials:

- Two copies of Lesson 21 Images page 1
- Scissors
- Tape
- Sheet of red paper
- Sheet of white paper

Lesson 21 Outline

1. Welcome music/gather to carpets

2. Welcome song: "The More We Get Together"

3. Attention grabber: Do What I'm Doing
   Skill: following directions

4. Calendar time
   Skills: patience, taking turns

5. Story time: *Where Do Diggers Sleep at Night?* by Brianne Caplan Sayers
   Skill: attention span

6. Transition activity: "The Wheels on the Bus"
   Skills: gross motor, music appreciation

7. Lesson: Which Vehicle Is Mine?
   Skills: critical thinking, imaginative play, patience

8. Hands-on activity: Pin the Ladder on the Fire Truck
   Skills: imaginative play, leadership, taking turns, teamwork

9. Theme song

10. Children dismissed for free play

Lesson 21 Details

Teacher Tip: Analyze Your Nonverbal Communication

This week, analyze how you are communicating with preschoolers not only verbally, but nonverbally as well. Your position (down on their level), spatial awareness, and use of personal space are powerful examples to children. Are you doing the activities along with the children? It is very important that you do! Children learn by example, so play right along with them. Use eye contact, hand gestures, and facial expression when talking with them. When speaking, always strive for positive interaction by using patience, empathy, respect, acceptance, and courteousness.

Transition Activity: "The Wheels on the Bus"

Skills: gross motor, music appreciation

Sing "The Wheels on the Bus" (#17 on the **LMG SUGGESTED SONG LIST**) while doing the actions.

Lesson: Which Vehicle Is Mine?

Skills: critical thinking, imaginative play, patience

1. Before the lesson, prepare the following:
    a. Use **tape** to hang pictures of various occupational vehicles (**Lesson 21 Images pages 2–5**) on the opposite side of the room. (The vehicles are a fire truck, police car, ambulance, tractor, excavator, and rocket.)
    b. Hang pictures of various locations (**Lesson 21 Images pages 5-8**) in different parts of your home or room. If possible, hang the pictures within seeing distance of the children but in all different locations. (The locations are a fire station, police station, hospital, farm, constructions site, and outer space.)

2. During the lesson, have each child take turns picking **a prop that represents the different occupations: firefighter, police officer, doctor, farmer, construction worker, and astronaut**. Have the child then cross the room to the vehicle photos in a creative way that represents that occupation. (Firefighters could crawl under smoke, police officers could sneak or tiptoe, astronauts jump or walk like they are on the moon, etc.)

3. Once he has crossed the room, have him choose which vehicle belongs to him. (Ex: If he has the firefighter prop, he will find the photo of the fire truck.) Help him tape that photo to his shirt.

4. Hand him **a steering wheel (a round household object, like a plate)** and tell him to drive to the picture of his vehicle's home. (Ex: If he is a firefighter driving a fire truck, he will need to find the fire station and "park" his vehicle there.)

5. When applicable, encourage him to make noises like his vehicle. Ask him to think through how his vehicle might sound and come up with an idea on his own. Help him as needed, but allow him to critically think about how to translate his thoughts into sounds. (Ex: If he is a firefighter pretending to drive a fire truck, he can make siren noises.)

6. If attention span allows, talk about something unique about each vehicle (rockets don't have wheels, a fire truck has a ladder and hose, etc.).

Hands-on Activity: Pin the Ladder on the Fire Truck

Skills: critical thinking, expressive language, fine motor, memory

1. Before the activity, print out one copy of the fire truck picture (**Lesson 21 Images page 1**) and leave as is. Print out a second copy of the image and use **scissors** to cut out several or all of the parts of the fire truck that don't make up the main body (ladder, wheels, siren, windows, hose, etc.). Place pieces of **tape** on the back of each piece of the fire truck, and put the pieces aside. Trace the remaining body of the fire truck onto your **red paper**. Cut it out and mount onto a **sheet of white paper**, creating a red silhouette of the fire truck that the children can fill in.

2. Show the children the complete image of the fire truck. Help them focus on the details. (Ex: "Where is the ladder? Why is it there? How is it used? Why is it needed?") Tell them to try and remember where each piece is located on the fire truck.

3. After they have studied the image and you have discussed the details together, take the completed picture away, and pull out the silhouette.

4. One at a time, have each child pick a piece of the fire truck (ex: the ladder) and choose where on the fire truck the ladder should go. Have him tape the piece on the correct part of the fire truck. After everyone has had a turn, bring out the original photo and compare. Repeat the activity if they are interested.

5. If time allows, play "Pin the Ladder on the Fire Truck" by following the rules of "Pin the Tail on the Donkey." Blindfold the child and let them try to stick one of the pieces in the right place.

Lesson 21 Outing and Parental Supplement

Outing: Vehicles at Work

Skills: curiosity, social-emotional development

Pick a vehicle that the children were particularly interested in during the lesson, and visit a location where they can see that vehicle at work. (Ex: see tractors at a farm, see rockets at a space museum/center, or see police cars at a station.)

Parental Supplement

Books:

- Any nonfiction book about occupational vehicles
- *Kids Meet the Emergency and Rescue Vehicles* by Andra Serlin Ambramson
- *Big Book of Rescue Vehicles* by Caroline Bingham
- *Mike Mulligan and His Steam Shovel* by Virginia Lee Burton
- *Whose Vehicle Is This?* by Sharon Katz Cooper
- *Grandpa's Tractor* by Michael Garland
- *Where Do Diggers Sleep at Night?* by Brianna Caplan Sayers
- *Busy, Busy Town* by Richard Scarry

Activities:

- Print out a picture of an occupational vehicle and let him color it. Cut the page out in puzzle shapes, and put it back together! This helps your child with fine motor skills (coloring) and pre-math skills (putting together a puzzle).
- Pretend with your child that you are riding together in an occupational vehicle of his choice. Where are you going? What will you do when you get there? What is your job? What can your vehicle do to help you?
- Take a drive and see how many occupational vehicles you can find.
- Make a matching game or a bingo card with occupations and occupational vehicles. Play games together.

Discussion:

- Ask your child which vehicle was his favorite? Why?
- Talk about the noises each one makes. Why do they make those noises?
- Say, "I'm thinking of a vehicle that _____." See if your child can guess based on your clues. Let him try to do the same for you!

Resources Used by Authors
- www.clker.com

Unit 4: Things That Move
Lesson 22: Cars, Trucks, and Automobiles

Lesson Objective: Have fun with toy cars while introducing the children to principles of basic science.

Lesson 21 Skill Objectives:

- Creativity
- Critical thinking
- Curiosity
- Decision making
- Expressive language
- Gross motor
- Imaginative play
- Patience
- Persistence
- Sensory development
- Social-emotional development
- Sportsmanship
- Taking turns
- Visual tracking

Preparation

Lesson Materials:

- At least two tracks on which to race toy cars*
- Several toy cars, preferably different colors

*If you don't already own tracks, they can be made from cardboard boxes, wood planks, or paper towel rolls cut in half lengthwise and taped together.

Hands-on Activity Materials:

- Shaving cream
- Several cookie sheets
- Toy cars and trucks
- Bowls of water
- Towels

Lesson 22 Outline

1. Welcome music/gather to carpets

2. Welcome song: "The More We Get Together"

3. Attention grabber: Hocus Pocus, Everybody Focus!
   Skill: visual tracking

4. Calendar time
   Skills: patience, taking turns

5. Story time: Picture books of your choice
   (Find any picture books at your local library about different types of cars, trucks, and other automobiles. This week, instead of having the children sit and listen to a story, look through the pictures together. Let them go at their own pace, and don't worry about how many pages they cover.)
   Skills: curiosity, decision making

6. Transition activity: Drive around the Room
   Skills: gross motor, imaginative play

7. Lesson: Race!
   Skills: critical thinking, expressive language, persistence, sportsmanship

8. Hands-on activity: Car Wash
   Skills: creativity, imaginative play, sensory development

9. Theme song

10. Children dismissed for free play

Lesson 22 Details

Teacher Tip: Teach Healthy Principles of Competition

This lesson is a good time to teach children healthy principles of competition. Do not emphasize winning and losing, but if the children start to notice, teach them healthy emotional principles. Praise each child for her efforts and strengths! Don't allow children to put each other down or be unkind. Help the children learn how to build each other up. Make it a fun, safe, and growing experience for all of the children.

Transition Activity: Drive around the Room

Skills: gross motor, imaginative play

Talk about the many types of cars, trucks, and other automobiles (like semitrucks, cars, pick-up trucks, or racecars). Have the children pretend to drive around the room. Ask them what automobile they are pretending to drive. Talk about how these automobiles drive differently, make different sounds, go fast or slow, etc. Also use this time to teach them about three basic parts of a vehicle: engine, wheels, and brakes. You could have them pretend to start their engines and step on the brakes!

Lesson: Race!

Skills: critical thinking, expressive language, persistence, sportsmanship

7. Before the lesson, set up at least **two tracks** on which the children will race toy cars. (If you don't already own tracks, they can be made from cardboard boxes, wood planks, or paper towel rolls cut in half lengthwise and taped together.)

8. Have each child pick a **toy car**. Instruct the children to look at their cars carefully and observe how they are similar or different from the other cars. Have each child describe her car to the rest of the class (like Show and Tell).

9. Group the children according to the number of tracks you have. (If you have two tracks, you'll have children race two at a time; three tracks, and the children will race three at a time.) Have them predict (make a *hypothesis*) about which car will be the fastest. Emphasize that the car will win or lose, and not the child. This is meant to be a fun experiment, and the children should be learning to ask questions, test, and analyze. (Ex: Say, "The BLUE car will be the fastest!" not "Claire's car will the fastest!")

10. After the race, review the experiment. Ask, "Were our guesses correct?" Try this process several times, and allow the children to switch cars. In the end, decide as a class which car was the fastest. Allow free time for racing and playing at the conclusion of the lesson.

Hands-on Activity: Car Wash

Skills: creativity, imaginative play, sensory development

Spray **shaving cream** on several **cookie sheets** Encourage the children to feel the shaving cream and spread the "bubbles" around to get ready for their car wash. Let them choose some **toy cars and trucks** to wash, and allow them to play freely, get creative, and be messy. Have **bowls of water** for rinsing and **towels** for drying cars (and kids!).

Lesson 22 Outing and Parental Supplement

Outing: Auto Museum, Car Show, Car Lot, or Racetrack

Skills: curiosity, social-emotional development

Visit an auto museum, car show, car lot, or racetrack. If you do not have anything like this in your area, go somewhere with bumper cars, ask a friend who owns several types of vehicles if you can come for a car tour, or go somewhere you can watch cars drive by.

Parental Supplement

Books:

- Any nonfiction books about vehicles
- *Cars: Rushing! Honking! Zooming!* by Patricia Hubbell
- *Trucks: Whizz! Zoom! Rumble!* by Patricia Hubbell
- *Dig Dig Digging* by Margaret Mayo
- *Cool Cars* by Tony Mitton
- *Little Blue Truck Leads the Way* by Alice Shertle
- *Cars Galore* by Peter Stein
- *If I Built a Car* by Chris Van Dusen

Activities:

- Paint with your toy cars. Dip the wheels in paint and "drive" them on paper. Compare their tire tracks then give them a car wash (see the hands-on activity). This also encourages children to help clean their toys.
- Draw a maze on the sidewalk, or make one inside with tape on the floor. See if your child can drive her cars through the maze.
- If you have a toy truck at home, see how many smaller things (like blocks or balls) it can hold. Use this as a counting exercise.
- Take your car through a car wash, or wash it together by hand.
- Ride on a bus.
- If you have food trucks in your area, go try some novelty foods.

Discussion:

- When you see cars or trucks on the road, discuss where they might be going. Ask, "What are the trucks carrying?"
- Count vehicles of the same color.
- Talk about the signs on the roads. What do they mean? How do they keep cars and trucks on the road safe?

Unit 4: Things That Move
Lesson 23: Planes, Trains, and Boats

Lesson Objective: Provide a sensory-rich play environment while encouraging sorting skills.

Lesson 23 Skill Objectives:

- Attention span
- Creativity
- Critical thinking
- Curiosity
- Fine motor
- Following directions
- Gross motor
- Imaginative play
- Individuality
- Patience
- Pre-math
- Problem solving
- Sensory development
- Taking turns
- Teamwork

Preparation

Lesson Materials:

- Blue blanket
- Masking tape
- Toy planes, trains, and boats*
- String, yarn, or wire
- Large bin filled with water**
- Large bin filled with dirt or sand**
- LMG SUGGESTED SONG LIST
- Toy train tracks (optional)

*You should preferably have enough planes, trains, and boats that each child can have one of each (just for the lesson—not to keep). If needed, we recommend borrowing toys from other parents in the group.

**These sensory bins can be reused by whomever is teaching Lesson 24.

Hands-on Activity Materials:

- Cardboard box for each child***
- Butcher paper
- Tape or glue
- Paper plates or paper circles (four for each box)
- Crayons, stickers, or other decorating supplies
- Rope or yarn
- Walking rope

*** Each cardboard box should be big enough that a child can wear it over his shoulders. (Diaper boxes are an excellent size.) If needed, have parents provide the children with boxes.

Lesson 23 Outline

1. Welcome music/gather to carpets

2. Welcome song: "The More We Get Together"

3. Attention grabber: Hands on Top, That Means Stop!
   Skill: following directions

4. Calendar time
   Skills: patience, taking turns

5. Story time: Picture books of your choice
   (Find any picture books at your local library that have beautiful photographs of planes, trains, or boats, like *The Big Book of Planes* or *The Big Book of Trains* by D.K. Publishing. Look through the pictures together.)
   Skills: attention span, curiosity

6. Transition activity: How Many Ways Can You Move?
   Skills: creativity, following directions, gross motor, individuality

7. Lesson: Planes, Trains, and Boats
   Skills: critical thinking, pre-math, problem solving, sensory development

8. Hands-on activity: Make a Train
   Skills: creativity, fine motor, gross motor, imaginative play, teamwork

9. Theme song

10. Children dismissed for free play

Lesson 23 Details

Teacher Tip: Teach Social Skills

This preschool setting is a great place to help children develop social skills. At their age, social skills include sharing, taking turns, and managing emotions. Children will not be naturally inclined to share or react to their feelings appropriately. During free time, monitor the play, and walk the children through potential conflicts. (Ex: "Hudson is playing with that toy right now. Clark, please ask him if you can have a turn when he is done." Or, "Hitting is not a kind way to tell your friends you are upset. How could you tell them?")

Transition Activity: How Many Ways Can You Move?

Skills: creativity, following directions, gross motor, individuality

Since this unit is about things that move, have each child take a turn showing everyone how his body can move. Each child gets to choose an action, and then everyone else follows. (You might want to demonstrate a few options so the children understand the expectation. Emphasize high-energy actions involving big movements, like jumping up and down, bouncing your head and shaking your hands, doing jumping jacks, somersaulting, running in place, and waving your arms up and down.)

Lesson: Planes, Trains, and Boats

Skills: critical thinking, pre-math, problem solving, sensory development

1. Before the lesson, prepare the following:
    a. Lay a **blue blanket** on the floor (to represent water).
    b. Use **masking tape** to create a track or route on the ground around the room (to represent train tracks). You will also need this track for the hands-on activity.

2. Also before the lesson, in a separate location from the blanket and masking tape, set up the following three stations. (These stations can be inside or outside, but they should be within sight of each other.)
    a. Station 1: Hang several **toy planes, trains, and boats** with **string, yarn, or wire** at the children's eye level. The toys should hang freely so they appear to be flying if you blow on them or swing them. (We strung yarn between two chairs and hung the toys from that.)
    b. Station 2: Place several trains, planes, and boats in a **large bin filled with water**. It's all right if the planes and trains sink to the bottom, but choose toy boats that will float.

c. Station 3: Place several trains, planes, and boats in a **large bin filled with sand or dirt**.

3. Introduce today's lesson with some songs.
    a. Sit on the blue blanket and pretend to row boats while you listen to or sing "Row, Row, Row Your Boat" (#19 on the **LMG SUGGESTED SONG LIST**).
    b. Have the children walk in a line on the taped track and pretend to be trains as you listen to or sing "I've Been Working on the Railroad" (#20 on the LMG SUGGESTED SONG LIST).
    c. Ask the children where the planes would go—on the "water" (blue blanket) or on the "track"? Pretend to fly around the room while listening to "The Airplane Song" (#21 on the LMG SUGGESTED SONG LIST).

4. Move to the three stations. Tell the children that today they are going to learn about things that move in the air, in the water, and on land. Clearly explain that the hanging strings represent air, the water bin represents water, and the sand/dirt bin represents land.
    a. Ask them if the vehicles are in the right places. Allow them to move all of the trains to the land and the boats to the water, and help them attach the planes to the strings.
    b. Talk about each vehicle and why it can function only in the correct environment. Ask critical-thinking questions as you discuss which vehicles fly, float, drive, etc. (Ex: Planes have wings, so they can fly in the air, but boats and trains can not.)
    c. The purpose of the bins is to provide a sensory station for the children to play in. It may come up (especially with preschoolers who love to play with trains) that trains drive on tracks, not just in the dirt. Feel free to provide **train tracks** for the children to place in the bin.

5. After you've helped them correctly sort each vehicle into its correct location, you can either repeat the mix-up game or allow free time to play with the sensory bins.

Hands-on Activity: Make a Train

Skills: creativity, fine motor, gross motor, imaginative play, teamwork

1. Before the children arrive, cut off the top and bottom of each **cardboard box**. (For a faster hands-on activity, also do step 2 before the children arrive.)

2. With the children's help, wrap each box in **butcher paper**. You can make each train car the same color or have several different colors to choose from.

3. Use **tape or glue** to attach **four paper plates or paper circles** to the bottom of each train car to make wheels. (Safety note: If you choose to use hot glue, make sure you teach children safety around the hot glue. Do not allow them to operate the glue gun or get burned.)

4. Allow the children to decorate their train cars. They can color with **crayons** or decorate with **stickers or other decorating supplies**. Cut two holes in both the front and back panels of each box. String **rope or yarn** through the holes so that each child can hold/wear his train car over his shoulders.

5. When everyone's train car is ready, line up and form a train. Have everyone hold onto the **walking rope** to stay connected. Assign one child to be the engine in front and one child to be the caboose in the back. Follow the taped track that was used earlier in the lesson. After driving in this order for a while, switch and give different children opportunities to be at different places in the train.

6. Play with different speeds, having your "engine car" lead. (Ex: "The train is picking up speed! It's going faster and faster! The train is slowing down now. How slow can you go? The train is stopping at the station now!")

7. Allow each child to take his train car home.

Lesson 23 Outing and Parental Supplement

Outing: The Airport

Skills: curiosity, gross motor

Visit a local airport. Small airports often have a place where you can safely have a great view of planes taking off and landing. Large airports sometimes have great views of the planes from the top of parking garages. Other options include taking a public transit train, going to a train park, or watching boats if you live near water. (Safety note: If you watch boats, make sure to review water safety, and never go near water without being in arm's reach of the children at all times.)

Parental Supplement

Books:

- Any nonfiction books about planes, trains, or boats
- *Locomotive* by Brian Floca
- *Airplanes: Soaring! Diving! Turning!* by Patricia Hubbell
- *Boats: Speeding! Sailing! Cruising!* by Patricia Hubbell
- *Trains: Steaming! Pulling! Huffing!* by Patricia Hubbell
- *The Little Airplane* by Lois Lenski
- *Toy Boat* by Loren Long
- *Amazing Airplanes* by Tony Mitton
- *Busy Boats* by Tony Mitton
- *Terrific Trains* by Tony Mitton
- *The Boat Alphabet Book* by Jerry Pallotta
- *The Little Engine That Could* by Watty Piper

Activities:

- Make paper boats. (You can find easy tutorials online.) Let your child help with the folding, and then float the boats in a bathtub or pool. Optional: Make a sail for your boat from a straw and a piece of paper. Give your child another straw, and let him be the "wind" and blow the boat around. Talk about how boats have different ways of moving (sails, motors, oars, etc.).
- Make paper airplanes together and see how far they can fly.
- If you have a train set at home, build tracks together and play.
- Use the cardboard train car from this week's activity, and add a steering wheel, wings, or anything else to make it into any kind of vehicle you'd like.
- Play the "sink or float" game. Fill a deep, clear container with water. Gather some toys and objects from around the house. Let your child guess which things will sink and which will float.

Discussion:
- In simple terms, point out the differences between things that float, sink, and fly.
- Where appropriate, throw items such as rocks, feathers, and leaves in puddles or ponds together. Before throwing an item, have your child guess whether it will sink or float. Notice together things that fly, float, or sink. Talk about why things that sink need to be on land, rather than on water.
- Ask, "Which one do you think is faster? A train? A plane? A boat?"
- Talk about different places you want to go together. When and why would you take a train? How about a plane? How about a boat? This would be a fun time to get out a map and show children how to get from place to place.
- Which of the three would you like to ride on the most? Why?
- Talk about other things that fly (like helicopters and hot air balloons) or travel in the water (like submarines). How are they different from the things we've already learned about? How are they the same?

Unit 4: Things That Move
Lesson 24: Forces of Nature

Lesson Objective: Learn how the water, ground, and air can move to create forces of nature, like tornadoes, earthquakes, and waves, using a variety of sensory activities.

Lesson 24 Skill Objectives:

- Attention span
- Critical thinking
- Fine motor
- Following directions
- Gross motor
- Patience
- Safety
- Sensory development
- Social-emotional development
- Taking turns

Preparation

Lesson Materials:

- Empty one-liter soda bottles (one for each child)
- Oil
- Water
- Blue food coloring
- Glue or tape
- Large bin of water
- Large bin of sand or dirt
- Straws (one for each child)
- Small toy that can float
- Cotton ball
- Toys or blocks
- Piece of paper or pillow
- Balloons (one for each child)

Hands-on Activity Materials:

- Water
- Tempera paint
- Straw (one for each child)
- Paper

Parent Responsibility:

- Shirt child can paint in

Lesson 24 Outline

1. Welcome music/gather to carpets

2. Welcome song: "The More We Get Together"

3. Attention grabber: One, Two, Three, Now Follow Me!
   Skill: following directions

4. Calendar time
   Skills: patience, taking turns

5. Story time: *Like a Windy Day* by Frank and Devin Asch
   Skills: attention span, curiosity

6. Transition activity: Tornado
   Skill: gross motor

7. Lesson: Forces of Nature
   Skills: critical thinking, fine motor, gross motor, safety, sensory development

8. Hands-on activity: Straw-Blown Paintings
   Skills: fine motor, sensory development

9. Theme song

10. Children dismissed for free play

Lesson 24 Details

Teacher Tip: Engage the Senses

Children love sensory activities, the value of which cannot be overstated. During this lesson, allow the children to play in the dirt/sand bin and water bin. Allowing children to touch, feel, explore, play with their hands, and use all their senses exposes them to new things, helps their brains make connections, and makes learning a lot of fun too!

Transition Activity: Tornado

Skill: gross motor

Talk about how the wind moves in many ways. Sometimes it moves really fast, starts spinning and swirling, and even picks up things like cars and houses! Have the children take turns pretending to be tornadoes by spinning as they pick up and drop toys. (Safety note: Don't let them run into anything or throw toys.)

Lesson: Forces of Nature

Skills: critical thinking, fine motor, gross motor, safety, sensory development

1. Before the lesson, prepare the following:
    a. Create a "wave bottle" for each child. Fill one-third of an **empty one-liter soda bottle** with **oil** and other two-thirds with **water**. Add **blue food coloring**. Secure the lid with **glue or tape**.
    b. Place **the large bin of water** and **the large bin of sand or dirt** in an area that can get wet and dirty. (Either get the bins from the teacher who taught Lesson 23 or make your own.)

2. Explain that this lesson is about the way water, the ground, and the wind move. Pass out a **straw** to each child. Practice blowing through the straws (NOT sucking). (They will need the straw at different points throughout the lesson.)

3. How water moves
    a. Put a **small toy that can float** in the water bin. Have each child take a turn trying to move the toy by making waves (by tipping, shifting, or nudging the bin).
    b. Talk about how some waves are caused from earthquakes that happen out in the ocean. With the earth and water moving at the same time, these waves tend to be very big!

    c. Try and move the toy by blowing through the straw (create "wind"). Tell them that waves are caused by the wind.
    d. Pass out the wave bottles. Explain that water also moves in waves. Waves roll and then crash on the shore. See if the children can make the waves roll in their bottles. (They can take these bottles home with them.)

4. How the ground moves
    a. Put a **cotton ball** in the dirt/sand bin. Have each child take a turn trying to move the ball by creating an earthquake (by tipping, shifting, or nudging the bin). Explain that the ground moves during an earthquake.
    b. Try moving the cotton ball by blowing through the straws to create wind. Tell them that wind is how air moves. Talk about dust storms and tornadoes. Explain that if the wind blows hard enough, it can lift the dirt/sand into the air. (Safety note: Before trying this, explain that the children need to be careful not to get sand in their eyes. Monitor this activity closely.)
    c. Set up some **toys** or stack **blocks** on a **piece of paper or pillow** (or something else you will be able to shake). After the children have built their towers, have them shake the paper or pillow and start an "earthquake." Watch as the toys or blocks fall.

5. How air moves
    a. Blow up a **balloon** for each child. Talk about how each balloon is filled with air.
    b. Play a game with a balloon: try to keep it off the ground by hitting it into the air and chasing it wherever it goes.

Hands-on Activity: Straw-Blown Paintings

Skills: fine motor, sensory development

Before you start, reemphasize the importance of blowing air out of the straw and not sucking up paint into the straw. (To reduce this risk, you can also cut a small hole near the top of the straw.) **Water** down **tempera paint** so that it is liquid enough to move when a **straw** is blown over it. Have the children don their **paint shirts**, let them pick their colors, and create beautiful art by blowing the paint across the **paper** with a straw. They may also discover that they can drip paint with the straw or write with the straw as well. Everyone's artwork will look wonderfully unique!

Lesson 24 Outing and Parental Supplement

Outing: Fly Kites

Skills: gross motor, sensory development, social-emotional development

Fly kites together. You may need to check the weather forecast and adjust your outing day to a time when there is wind. If there is no wind during this time, get together at home and use a water table to observe how water *flows*. (If you don't own a water table, you can use a large container, plastic bin, or kiddie pool filled with a few inches of water.) Pour the water using measuring cups, drop things into the water (to see ripples), or swirl the water with a toy (to see how the water and any floating toys keep moving in circles before slowing down). You can also play the sink or float game and see which objects sink and which ones float.

Parental Supplement

Books:

- Any issue of *Children's National Geographic* focusing on forces of nature such as earthquakes, volcanoes, ocean tides, hurricanes, or tornados
- *Like a Windy Day* by Frank and Devin Asch
- *One Small Place by the Sea* by Barbara Brenner
- *I Face the Wind* by Vicki Cobb
- *Feel the Wind* by Arthur Dorros

Activities:

- Make a tornado in a jar. Fill a jar with water and a few drop of soap. Put the lid on. Shake, swirl, and watch for the tornado!
- Play with the wave bottles the children brought home from class.
- Guess which way the wind is blowing by watching the movement of the trees, clouds, etc.
- Make a pinwheel.
- Play with a water table. See this lesson's outing for ideas.
- Make homemade wind chimes from household items, like empty tin cans. Talk about the different sounds we hear and how the wind chimes work because of the movement of the wind.
- If you live close to a body of water, go watch the waves or stay long enough to see the tide change.
- Eat a gelatin snack and let the child create an "earthquake" and watch it jiggle.
- Find a trampoline park, bounce house, home trampoline, or open gym in your area. Talk about how the ground is moving as they jump. Relate it to earthquakes.

Discussion:
- Talk about the *tide* and tide pools.
- Almost all of the ways that the forces of nature move can be dangerous. Talk about principles of safety when dealing with waves, winds, earthquakes, tornadoes, etc.
- If you have sand dunes or wind caves in your area, talk about how they formed.
- Watch and discuss the weather.

Unit 4: Things That Move
Lesson 25: Solar System

Lesson Objective: Learn about our solar system in a fun and interactive way.

Lesson 25 Skill Objectives:

- Attention span
- Creativity
- Decision making
- Fine motor
- Following directions
- Gross motor
- Music appreciation
- Patience
- Taking turns

Preparation

Transition Activity Materials:

- LMG SUGGESTED SONG LIST

Lesson Materials:

- Nine paper circles of different sizes and colors representing the sun and eight planets
- Lesson 25 Images (as a reference)
- Scissors
- Yarn
- Tape
- Large, empty wall in your home

Hands-on Activity Materials:

- Sugar cookies in various sizes
- Frosting in several different colors

Parent Responsibility:

- Shirt child can frost cookies in

Lesson 25 Outline

1. Welcome music/gather to carpets

2. Welcome song: "The More We Get Together"

3. Attention grabber: Stand Up! Sit Down.
   Skills: following directions, gross motor

4. Calendar time
   Skills: patience, taking turns

5. Story time: *The Sun: Our Nearest Star* by Franklyn M. Branley
   Skill: attention span

6. Transition activity: "Planets Song"
   Skill: gross motor, music appreciation

7. Lesson: Our Solar System
   Skills: decision making, fine motor, gross motor, teamwork

8. Hands-on activity: Solar System Cookies
   Skills: creativity, fine motor

9. Theme song

10. Children dismissed for free play

Lesson 25 Details

Teacher Tip: Focus on the Wonder

The solar system is an abstract concept and complex subject that preschoolers will not be able to fully grasp. Try your best to build upon their prior knowledge and explain the topics in the lesson. However, remember that our focus is making them excited about learning, rather than ensuring they'll retain information. Don't worry about how much they remember or understand. Instead, focus on the experience they are having. Help instill a sense of fascination, curiosity, and wonder into their little minds!

Transition Activity: "Planets Song"

Skill: gross motor, music appreciation

Dance together to "Planets Song" (#18 on the **LMG SUGGESTED SONG LIST**).

Lesson: Our Solar System

Skills: decision making, fine motor, gross motor, teamwork

1. Before the lesson, prepare the following:
    a. Print or cut out **nine paper circles of different sizes and colors** to represent each of the eight planets and the sun. For a reference of general sizes and colors of the planets, see **Lesson 25 Images**.
        i. The eight planets go in the following order: Mercury, Venus, Earth, Mars, Jupiter, Saturn, Uranus, and Neptune.
        ii. Some teachers may remember when Pluto was counted as a ninth planet, but the latest information states that it is a "dwarf planet" and technically not part of our solar system. You can choose whether to mention Pluto or not.
    b. Use **scissors** to cut eight pieces of **yarn** into progressively longer pieces. **Tape** one end of each yarn piece to the planets in order of distance from the sun (i.e. Mercury's yarn should be the shortest, and Neptune's should be the longest.) There will be no yarn attached to the sun.
    c. Put a piece of tape on the back of each planet, and arrange the planets on the floor (in random order) in front of a **large, empty wall of your home**. Have more tape ready for the lesson.

2. Point to the blank wall and tell the children that we are going to make the wall into our solar system.

a. Review what you learned in today's story about the sun being the center. Ask one of the children to put the sun in the center of the wall. (You might have to assist him to make sure it's in the center, but let him try first.)
   b. Have the children take turns choosing a planet to tape to the wall. In each case, help them first tape their loose end of string to the sun and then pull their string tight before securing their planet. They can tape the planet any direction from the sun that they would like. (Because the strings are increasingly longer, the final product should be an accurate representation of the solar system, no matter where the children taped their planets.)
   c. Make sure to emphasize some basic information, such as the fact that earth is the planet we live on, the sun is what keeps us warm, or it would be very cold on Neptune.

3. Explain that each planet *orbits* around the sun. Some planets are closer to the sun than others, so they go around the sun more quickly. Further planets take longer to go all the way around the sun. Act out the solar system with the following activity:
   a. Find a space that is large enough for a lot of movement. Have each child pick a planet that he wants to be, or assign them each a planet. (You can make them nametags, tape the circles from the lesson to their chests, or simply tell them which they are assigned to be.)
   b. Based on your assignments, explain how close or far away their "orbit" will be. (Optional: Ahead of time, tape circles on the floor to represent the different orbits.)
   c. Stand in the center and tell them that you are the sun. Have them run as fast as they can around their circle while staying "in orbit". This will test their balance, concentration, and teamwork.
   d. Have them change orbits if they would like. Take rests so they don't get too dizzy.
   e. If your children are up for a challenge, teach them that planets spin as they orbit. See if they can spin while they still move in orbit!

Hands-on Activity: Solar System Cookies

Skills: creativity, fine motor

Before the lesson, bake some **sugar cookies in varying sizes** to represent the sun and eight planets. Let them cool. During the lesson, help the children **frost** the appropriate cookies with colors corresponding to your wall diagram. (Make sure they are wearing **shirts they can frost cookies in**.) Lay the cookies out in the order of the solar system together! Enjoy eating the cookies.

Optional: Roll out cookie dough for the children, and let them cut out cookies in several different sizes. (Your sun and larger planets will probably need to be bigger than cookie cutters will allow.) While the cookies bake, let the children help you decide what colors to make the frosting. Proceed with the instructions above. (Safety note: Children should not to go near the oven or help with the baking part of the lesson.)

Lesson 25 Outing and Parental Supplement

Outing: Planetarium

Skills: curiosity, social-emotional development

Go to a local planetarium together. If you don't have access to a planetarium in your area, you could find a space museum, launch model rockets or stomp rockets, or even consider having a nighttime outing and stargazing.

Parental Supplement

Books:

- *Countdown! with Milo* by Mike Austin
- *The Sun: Our Nearest Star* by Franklyn M. Branley
- *Papa, Please Get the Moon for Me* by Eric Carle
- *The Magic School Bus Lost in the Solar System* by Joanna Cole (advanced)
- *National Geographic Kids First Big Book of Space* by Catherine D. Hughes (advanced)
- *If You Decide to Go to the Moon* by Faith McNulty (advanced)
- *This Is a Moose* by Richard T. Morris
- *What's out There? A Book about Space* by Lynn Wilson (advanced)

Activities:

- Go outside together during the day and look up at the sky. What do you see? Where is the sun? What does it do? Make sure you point out that the sun is in a different place in morning than it is in the evening. Why is that? Are we moving, or is the sun? (Safety note: Make sure the child doesn't stare directly at the sun.)
- Go outside at nighttime and look up at the sky. What do you see? Where is the sun now? Where is the moon? What stars do you see?
- Use a globe (or a balloon or ball) to learn about day and night. In a dark room, shine a flashlight on the globe, and slowly spin it around. Put a sticker on the place where you live, and have your child follow it from light to dark. Talk about what happens when the earth spins. Where is it day, and where is it night?
- Use sidewalk chalk to draw planets and/or the solar system. Optional: Draw circles to represent the planets' orbits and play the orbit game from the lesson again.
- Launch model rockets, stomp rockets, or make homemade rockets at home with balloons. Be sure to practice counting down backwards before the blast off!

Discussion:

- Throughout the week, ask your child questions about what he learned about the solar system. See what he remembers and understood. Allow him to ask questions, but discuss the solar system only as long as he is interested and excited about it.
- Look through the suggested books and others you find together. Discuss what you see.
- Talk about rockets, spaceships, astronauts, and space travel.

Resources Used by Authors:
- www.clker.com

Unit 4: Things That Move
Lesson 26: You Move—I Can Hike and Play

Note: As a wrap-up to Unit 4 (Thing That Move), lessons 26 and 27 will focus completely on the children moving. For these two weeks only, we ask for full parental involvement on both days of the week. We eliminated all other parts of our usual lesson structure so the children could focus completely on movement, exercise, and play.

Lesson 26 Skill Objectives:

- Gross motor
- Healthy Habits
- Sensory development
- Sportsmanship
- Teamwork

Preparation

Materials:

- If necessary, borrow equipment suited to this age group

Parent Responsibility:

- Attend both days this week

Lesson 26 Details

Teacher Tip: Encourage Physical Activity

While physical activity is probably already a normal part of your preschooler's routine, we want to continue encouraging children and families to take advantage of opportunities to move, explore, and be active, especially outdoors. Although the pull of technology continues to increase, research consistently shows that preschoolers thrive on having experiences outdoors, where they can connect with nature and improve their balance and coordination. This can also boost brain development, enhance social skills, and improve their abilities to concentrate and perform well in school in later years. Fresh air, exercise, uneven terrain, new environments, and new challenges all aid in the healthy and important mental, physical, and emotional development of a preschool-aged child. Enjoy hiking, running, and playing together, knowing that you are building much more in their little minds and bodies than just a fun day on the trails.

Day 1: I Can Hike

Skills: gross motor, healthy habits, sensory development

Take the group on a hike or a walk anywhere you choose. Talk to them about how walking is healthy for our bodies and minds. Move at their pace, and enjoy the experience for as long as the children can tolerate and time allows.

Day 2: I Can Play

Skills: gross motor, healthy habits, sportsmanship, teamwork

1. Ideally this lesson will take place outdoors where there is plenty of space to run, like a field, backyard, or track. If weather conditions do not allow, consider a gymnasium or other indoor location with enough room for the children to run around.

2. Reemphasize the importance of keeping our bodies and minds healthy through movement and exercise. Also stress that moving is fun and makes us feel good. Do any of the following activities together, and add more of your own if you prefer!
    a. Run races! You could start with simple races in which the children have to run from point A to point B. You can also add more complicated races, such as the eraser race: each child has a pile of erasers (or other objects) at one end of the track and a mark at the other end of the track. Simultaneously, each racer runs down to the end of the track, picks up one object from her pile, places it at the

other end of the track, and repeats until she has moved all of her objects. The one to relocate her pile first wins.
   b. Play duck, duck, goose.
   c. Run a simple relay together. Teach them basic principles of teamwork. Some ideas for relay stations are hopping in a hoop, doing summersaults, walking on a line, spinning, etc. Start with one simple command, and build up to three commands in a row that the children must follow. Practicing a sequence of commands challenges them, strengthens their mental capacities, and improves ability to follow more complex instructions.

Lesson 26 Parental Supplement

Activity:
- Play actively with your child this week. Take walks, exercise, dance, or play active games together.

Discussion:
- Talk to your child about principles of teamwork and healthy competition.
- Talk to your child about keeping our minds and bodies healthy through movement.

Unit 4: Things That Move
Lesson 27: You Move—I Can Play Sports and Games

Note: As a wrap-up to Unit 4 (Thing That Move), lessons 26 and 27 will focus completely on the children moving. For these two weeks only, we ask for full parental involvement on both days of the week. We eliminated all other parts of our usual lesson structure so the children could focus completely on movement, exercise, and play.

Lesson 27 Skill Objectives:

- Gross motor
- Healthy habits
- Sensory development
- Sportsmanship
- Teamwork

Preparation

Materials:

- If necessary, borrow equipment suited to this age group

Parent Responsibility:

- Attend both days this week

Lesson 27 Details

Teacher Tip: Focus on Fun

While preschool may be too early to successfully have an organized sports game, recognize that this week's objective is to simply introduce some sporting techniques, while mainly focusing on movement and fun! Our advice is to keep it simple. Do as much as the children are interested in, but know that playing soccer at this age doesn't necessarily involve a formal game with goalies and points. The group may, however, be capable of kicking the ball back and forth or taking turns kicking the ball into a goal. For basketball, you might practice shooting or dribbling. Praise their efforts. Understand that the rules and specifics of these games are not what are important; rather, teach the basic concepts of each sport, integrate simple principles of teamwork and healthy attitudes about competition, and cultivate an overall attitude that moving and playing are fun and fulfilling!

Day 1: Soccer and Basketball

Skills: gross motor, healthy habits, sensory development, sportsmanship, teamwork

Teach the children basic principles of soccer and basketball. According to the needs of your group, choose whether you will split the children into teams or just have them practice kicking the ball (soccer) and shooting baskets (basketball) together. Spend about half of the time on each sport. Point out to the children that different sports require us to move in different ways. Soccer mostly requires using our legs, while basketball requires moving our arms, etc. Encourage children to cheer for each other's successes! (If you don't own the equipment for soccer and basketball, get creative! For example, use a pair of shoes for goalposts or a box instead of a basket.)

Day 2: T-Ball and Flag Football

Skills: gross motor, healthy habits, sensory development, sportsmanship, teamwork

Teach the children basic principles of baseball (T-ball) and flag football. (For our purposes, flag football is just a version of tag in which the children chase and try to tag the child with the ball. This is a very simple way to introduce the basics of football.) According to the needs of your group, choose whether you will split the children into teams or just have them all practice hitting the ball (T-ball) and running with the ball (flag football) together. Spend about half of the time on each sport.

Safety note: Bring plenty of water for the children, and talk about the importance of staying hydrated so our bodies can be healthy and continue to move.

Lesson 27 Parental Supplement

Activity:
- Play actively with your child this week. Take walks, exercise, dance, or play active games together.

Discussion:
- Talk to your child about principles of teamwork and healthy competition.
- Talk to your child about keeping our minds and bodies healthy through movement.

Unit 5: Things That Grow
Lesson 28: Types of Plants

Lesson Objective: Practice simple sorting and sequence skills while identifying different types of plants.

Lesson 28 Skill Objectives:

- Attention span
- Curiosity
- Fine motor
- Following directions
- Gross motor
- Imaginative play
- Patience
- Pre-math
- Problem solving
- Sensory development
- Social-emotional development
- Taking turns
- Teamwork

Preparation

Transition Activity Materials:

- Picture of a vine (optional)

Lesson Materials:

- Several copies of Lesson 28 Images, already cut out

Hands-on Activity Materials:

- Several blankets
- Pillows
- Chairs (to build a fort)
- Green balloons
- Tape
- Leaves and flowers cut from construction paper
- Green streamers

Lesson 28 Outline

1. Welcome music/gather to carpets

2. Welcome song: "The More We Get Together"

3. Attention grabber: Hands on Top, That Means Stop!
   Skills: following directions, gross motor

4. Calendar time
   Skills: patience, taking turns

5. Story time: *I Took a Walk* by Henry Cole
   Skill: attention span

6. Transition activity: Friendship Vine
   Skills: gross motor, taking turns, teamwork

7. Lesson: Plant Patterns
   Skills: attention span, critical thinking, pre-math

8. Hands-on activity: Rainforest Fort
   Skills: creativity, fine motor

9. Theme song

10. Children dismissed for free play

Lesson 28 Details

Teacher Tip: Exercise Imagination

The majority of today's material focuses on building a rainforest fort. This is a great opportunity to exercise imagination and promote free play, both of which are essential to the healthy development of preschool-aged children. If the lesson section ends quickly, that's all right. Spend time talking about the rainforest elements as you build the fort. Allow the children to continue to imagine and play in their newly created environment. Enjoy watching their excitement and imaginations grow!

Transition Activity: Friendship Vine

Skill: attention span, critical thinking, pre-math

Have two children hold hands (just one set of hands, leaving a free hand for each child) and tell them they are creating a *vine. (You may want to show them a **picture of a vine** so they better understand the concept.) As they grab the hands of other children around them, their vine grows. When they are all connected as one big vine, have them follow wherever the leader goes. Give each child a chance to be the leader!

Lesson: Plant Patterns

Skills: decision making, fine motor, gross motor, teamwork

1. Before the lesson, make several copies of each of the four **Lesson 28 Images**. Cut them out, and lay them face-up on the floor in random order.

2. Begin by asking the children if they can identify any of the pictures that they see. Once they have successfully done so, challenge them to pick out all of the pictures of that type. (Ex: If they first identify the flower picture, have them pick out all of the flower pictures and put them in a pile.) Practice this simple sorting activity with each of the four types of plants until you have sorted the images into four different piles.

3. Tell the children that they are going to play a new game. Lay out a few pictures in a simple pattern (ex: grass, tree, grass). Ask which comes next (ex: tree). After a child has answered correctly, hand her the correct picture to put in the sequence. Repeat using a different pattern, and give each child a chance to answer. Begin with very simple patterns, and make them more complex if the children grasp the concept.

Hands-on Activity: Rainforest Fort

Skills: gross motor, imaginative play

1. Tell the children about a place called the *rainforest, a type of jungle. Explain that this is a place where plants grow everywhere. They will learn about different types of plants in the rainforest by building their own rainforest fort!

2. Teach them that the bottom of the rainforest has grasses and weeds. They don't grow very tall. They stay at the bottom, where it's dark and people and animals walk on them. Place a **blanket** on the ground and explain that it represents the grass/weeds on the floor of the jungle. Have the children crawl onto the "forest floor."

3. Explain that above the rainforest floor there are smaller plants like bushes, shrubs, and flowers. They grow taller than grass but not as tall as trees. They are good hiding places for insects and small animals. Place some **pillows** on the blanket and explain that the pillows represent the bushes and flowers.

4. Explain that trees in the rainforest grow tall so that the sun can shine on them. There are a lot of trees in the rainforest, and they grow so close together that their branches and leaves form a *canopy, a covering over the rainforest. Pull **chairs** around the edge of the blanket. (The chair legs can help hold the floor blanket in place.) Put **another blanket** (or blankets) over the top of the chairs. The chair legs represent the tree trunks, and the blanket on top represents the canopy.

5. To make the fort feel more like a rainforest, use **green balloons** as fun bushes or shrubs for the children to play with. **Tape** the **leaves and flowers cut from construction paper** to the chair legs. Have the children hang **green streamers** throughout the fort to represent jungle vines.

6. Allow the children to play in their rainforest fort as long as they would like. Point out the types of "plants" all around them, then let them play and use their imaginations!

Lesson 28 Outing and Parental Supplement

Outing: Botanical Garden

Skills: curiosity, gross motor, sensory development, social-emotional development

Visit a botanical garden together. If you don't have a botanical garden available in your area, go on a nature walk and have the children collect things they find along the way (leaves, pinecones, blossoms, sticks, etc.). When they get home, encourage them to make their findings into a collage or collection.

Parental Supplement

Books:

- *The Curious Garden* by Peter Brown
- *I Took a Walk* by Henry Cole
- *Jack's Garden* by Henry Cole
- *On Meadowview Street* by Henry Cole
- *My Garden* by Kevin Henkes

Activities:

- Press flowers in the pages of a book and leave them there to dry.
- Do a comparison exercise by having your child talk about plant types from smallest to biggest.
- Pull weeds at your house or at a neighbor's.
- Build a rainforest fort at home and review the types of plants. Play with your child in this setting. Use your imagination!

Discussion:

- What kinds of plants do you have around your house?
- When you are out walking, practice identifying the differences in plants that you see.
- How can plants help us? How can plants help animals? (Ex: Trees are places for birds to build their nests. Some animals eat plants. Some plants can help us feel better, like aloe. Trees provide shade.)
- If you have a lawn that requires mowing, point out that we have to cut the grass frequently because it grows so quickly. How does that compare to other types of plants in our yard or around our home?

Unit 5: Things That Grow
Lesson 29: How Plants Grow

Lesson Objective: Teach children the principles of caring for growing things, and prepare them to take responsibility for plants of their own.

Lesson 29 Skill Objectives:

- Accountability
- Attention span
- Critical thinking
- Curiosity
- Decision making
- Following directions
- Gross motor
- Music appreciation
- Patience
- Perseverance
- Problem solving
- Resourcefulness
- Responsibility
- Sensory development
- Social-emotional development
- Taking turns
- Teamwork

Preparation

Transition Activity Materials:

- Walking rope

Lesson Materials:

- Way to display images*
- Lesson 29 Images, cut out

*You can mount the images on felt and create your own flannel board by pinning, hot-gluing, or stapling felt to a whiteboard or bulletin board. You can also mount the images on magnets and stick them to your fridge or another magnetic surface, or simply cut out the images and tape them to a wall.

Hands-on Activity Materials:

- Pot for each child**
- Potting soil
- Packet of sunflower seeds
- Water
- Cup or watering can

**Sour cream containers, small jars, and paper cups all work well.

Lesson 29 Outline

1. Welcome music/gather to carpets

2. Welcome song: "The More We Get Together"

3. Attention grabber: Do What I'm Doing
   Skills: following directions, gross motor

4. Calendar time
   Skills: patience, taking turns

5. Story time: *And Then It's Spring* by Julie Fogliano
   Skill: attention span

6. Transition activity: I Spy . . . Signs of Spring!
   Skills: curiosity, gross motor, sensory development

7. Lesson: How Do Plants Grow?
   Skills: critical thinking, patience, perseverance, problem solving

8. Hands-on activity: Plant a Seed
   Skills: accountability, patience, perseverance, resourcefulness, responsibility

9. Theme song

10. Children dismissed for free play

Lesson 29 Details

Teacher Tip: Teach Patience and Responsibility

This week's material allows the children to begin a project (planting a seed) that requires patience—after all, several days will pass before they see any results! This is also a great opportunity to teach responsibility both in the classroom and at home. Encourage the children to care for their plants (even before they see signs of growth) and wait patiently for results. Developing patience and responsibility are life skills that allow for character building and increased emotional maturity.

Transition Activity: I Spy . . . Signs of Spring!

Skills: curiosity, gross motor, sensory development

If the weather allows, use your **walking rope** to take a short walk outside and look for signs of spring. Look for new leaves on the trees, grass starting to grow or turn green again, flowers starting to bud, or any other signs of life and growth. You may have to be a little creative, but with a little forethought and preparation, you are sure to find something around your home or neighborhood that represents growth. Help the children look for and discover these signs of spring for themselves.

Lesson: How Do Plants Grow?

Skills: critical thinking, patience, perseverance, problem solving

1. Before the lesson, choose how you will **display** your **Lesson 29 Images**. You can mount the images on felt and create your own flannel board by pinning, hot-gluing, or stapling felt to a whiteboard or bulletin board. You can also mount the images on magnets and stick them to your fridge or another magnetic surface, or simply cut out the images and tape them to a wall.
    a. Lay the images face-up on the carpet so the children can see them. Use the images to help them answer the lesson questions correctly.
    b. Be sure to cut the picture of the flower so that the stem and leaves are separate from the actual flower.

2. As you start the lesson, ask the children to review the different plants they learned about last week in Lesson 28. What kinds of plants can they remember? Which ones were their favorites?

3. Explain, "Today we are going to learn how plants grow. All things that are alive grow, including us. Do you remember what we need to live/grow from Unit 2?" (Answers will include sleep, food, movement, etc.) "Plants need some of the same things that we do to live and grow! Today we are going to learn about those things." (Feel free to adapt any of the following in-depth portions as needed to maintain attention spans.)

4. What is the first thing a plant needs so it can grow? Food!
    a. Plants need *nutrients*, or healthy food, to be able to grow, just like we do.
    b. Ask what they think a plant's favorite food is. The answer is *soil*, special dirt with lots of nutrients.
    c. Have one child place the image of soil on the board.
    d. Have another child take the image of the seed and "plant" it (place it) on the soil. Talk about how the seed is eating up the yummy soil all around it.

5. Next, the seed needs room to grow. Have the children look at your display to see if they think the seed has enough room to grow.
    a. There are plants we call *weeds* that grow faster than the beautiful flowers and plants we are trying to grow. Weeds can take up all of the space, leaving no room for our flowers.
    b. Place a few cutouts of weeds on the board. Ask the children what we should do to solve this problem. Let them figure out the solution for themselves, prompting them as needed. Let them take turns "pulling" the weeds.
    c. Throughout the rest of the lesson, add more weeds as the plant grows, and let them "pull" the weeds each time.

6. What does the plant need next? Water!
    a. Even though we did not specifically mention that we need water in Unit 2, we do! Ask them how they feel when they are hot and thirsty. Doesn't it make them feel so much better to get a big, refreshing drink of water?
    b. Have one of the children place the image of the watering can directly over the seed. Ask the children what they think is going to happen next.
    c. After the seed has been "watered," place the picture of the roots below the seed. Explain that a seed must grow roots before it is strong enough to pop out of the ground. The roots help the plant eat more nutrients and drink more water to get stronger.

7. What is the last thing the plant needs so it can grow? Sunlight!
    a. Just like us, plants love the sunshine. They will work hard to push out of the ground and grow towards the sunlight.
    b. Have one of the children place the sunshine directly above the seed. Ask the children what they think will happen. After they answer, put up the picture of the stem and leaves (not the flower itself).

c. Ask the children, "Have we done everything correctly? Have we given the flower everything it needs to grow?" (The answer is yes.) Ask them, "What do we still need to do so that our flower can continue to grow?" The answer is to continue to do all of these things! Explain that even though we have done all of the right things, it still takes time, patience, and work to help our flower grow.

8. Leaving the flower pieces that you have already "grown" on the board, review all of the steps again (food, room to grow, water, sunlight). Depending on interest level and attention span, you can repeat the cycle more than once. Don't forget to frequently add in weeds! After the children have continued to care for their plant and have demonstrated patience and perseverance, add the picture of the flower to the top of the plant. Praise them for their patience and hard work!

9. Take everything down and ask the children if they can recreate the "story" of the growing seed in order. Prompt them as needed, and allow them to take turns putting up the different pieces in the correct order.

10. Optional: As you play this game, or if it ends too quickly, play the "What If..." game, which will require them to think critically. Remind them of some of what they learned in today's story. There are several conditions that would make it difficult for a seed to grow.
    a. What would happen if we put this plant in the oven?
    b. What would happen if we put this plant in the freezer?
    c. What would happen if we put this plant in a dark room?
    d. What would happen if we didn't pull the weeds?
    e. What would happen if we forgot to water the plant?
    f. What would happen if we just put the seed on the kitchen counter?

Hands-on Activity: Plant a Seed

Skills: accountability, patience, perseverance, resourcefulness, responsibility

1. Explain to the children that they will have the opportunity to plant a seed of their very own! Remind them that they will be responsible for caring for their seed and making sure it has what it needs to grow into a beautiful flower.

2. Review what you learned in the lesson. What is the first thing a plant needs to live and grow? (Food/soil.) Without soil to give the plant food, the plant does not have the energy it needs to push its way up to the sunlight. Help each child fill his **pot** with **potting soil**.

3. Give each child a **sunflower seed**, and show him how to plant it at the proper depth. Remind the children that the seeds need to be deep enough to make roots but not so deep that they can't reach up to the sunlight.

4. After their seeds are planted, help them remember the last three things each plant needs to grow.
    a. **Water**. Have them each take turns watering their seed with a **cup or a watering can**.
    b. Sunlight. Show them how to find a sunny area of their home or backyard where the plant will get plenty of light to grow.
    c. Space to grow. Remind them that the flower's roots will start out very small, so the pot will provide plenty of space. Later, as the flower grows, their parents can help them find a bigger area in which to plant the flower, so it can continue to have the space it needs for its roots to spread out and grow.

Lesson 29 Outing and Parental Supplement

Outing: Greenhouse or Nursery

Skills: curiosity, gross motor, sensory development, social-emotional development

Visit a greenhouse or nursery to observe and discuss how the people there take care of the plants and help them grow. (Ex: They place the plants in places with sunlight, and they water the plants regularly.) If these locations aren't available in your area, visit the garden section of your local Walmart, Home Depot, etc.

Parental Supplement

Books:

- *The Curious Garden* by Peter Brown
- *Jack's Garden* by Henry Cole
- *How a Seed Grows* by Helene J. Jordan
- *The Carrot Seed* by Ruth Krauss
- *Dig and Sow! How Do Plants Grow?* by Janice Lobb (advanced)
- *How a Seed Grows into a Sunflower* by David Stewart (advanced)

Activities:

- Help your child take responsibility for his newly planted seed. Encourage him to care for it.
- If you have a garden at home, encourage your child to help you in the garden. Make sure you discuss together the principles of caring for a garden.
- Go on a walk together, looking for growing plants and flowers. Pay attention to whether the plants look healthy or not. Discuss what the plants might need more of in order to be healthy.
- Find a small space where you can plant something with your child (either in your yard or a planter). Let your child help decide what to plant.
- In addition to your child's newly planted flower, plant beans together in a plastic bag and watch the roots grow. Place the bean seeds in a reusable, re-sealable plastic bag with wet cotton balls. Tape the bag to the window, and make sure it remains moist inside as the beans grow. In only a few days, you will see the beans sprout, and you can watch the roots grow.
- Use a ruler to measure how tall your child's flower or other plants around your home are. (This is a great, simple introduction to measurement.)

Discussion:

- Discuss the ways that we can respect the plants around us to help keep our world beautiful. How can we take responsibility for keeping our world a beautiful place?
- See the "What If..." game in this week's lesson. Play it together as you talk about and care for your child's plant.
- Point out and discuss the differences in how fast certain plants grow in relation to others.

Resources Used by the Authors
- http://gardening.about.com/od/plantprofiles/p/Sunfflowers.htm
- www.clker.com

Unit 5: Things That Grow
Lesson 30: Leaves

Lesson Objective: Learn about how leaves help trees grow, while also reviewing seasons.

Lesson 30 Skill Objectives:

- Attention span
- Creativity
- Critical thinking
- Curiosity
- Fine motor
- Following directions
- Gross motor
- Imaginative play
- Music appreciation
- Patience
- Rhyming
- Sensory development
- Social-emotional development
- Taking turns

Preparation

Transition Activity Materials:

- Large bedsheet
- Artificial leaves, both green and autumn colors (bought from a craft store or cut from construction paper)

Lesson Materials:

- Large sheet of butcher paper
- Tape
- Artificial leaves, both green and autumn colors (bought from a craft store or cut from construction paper)
- Tree guide, book of trees, or tree encyclopedia with good pictures
- Garden rake (real or toy); get multiple rakes if possible
- Pillows or blankets

Hands-on Activity Materials:

- Brown paper
- White paper (one sheet for each child)
- Gold glitter
- Construction paper in different leaf colors
- Glue

Lesson 30 Outline

1. Welcome music/gather to carpets

2. Welcome song: "The More We Get Together"

3. Attention grabber: One, Two, Three, Now Follow Me!
   Skill: following directions

4. Calendar time
   Skills: patience, taking turns

5. Story time: *Leaves* by David Ezra Stein
   Skill: attention span

6. Transition activity: Parachute
   Skill: gross motor

7. Lesson: Leaves and Raking
   Skills: critical thinking, imaginative play, patience

8. Hands-on activity: Leaves on a Tree
   Skills: creativity, fine motor

9. Theme song

10. Children dismissed for free play

Lesson 30 Details

Teacher Tip: Enjoy the Great Outdoors

By the time you teach Unit 5, the weather in most areas should be starting to get warmer and more appropriate for being outside. Feel free to use your walking rope whenever you feel it could be beneficial for your group. You could also move parts of your lesson to an outdoor setting!

Transition Activity: Parachute

Skill: gross motor

Use a **large bedsheet** as a parachute and fill it with the **artificial leaves**. Have each child hold onto the sides of the sheet and move it up and down quickly, throwing leaves up into the air and hopefully down onto the children!

Lesson: Leaves and Raking

Skills: critical thinking, imaginative play, patience

1. Before the lesson, draw a very simple tree trunk (with branches coming off the top) on a **large sheet of butcher paper**. Make it about the height of your preschoolers, and **tape** it to the wall.

2. Explain the following while holding up the different-colored **artificial leaves** from the transition activity:
    a. Plants need leaves! Do you know why? The leaves soak up the sunlight and air to help the plants grow. What might happen to a tree if it lost all of its leaves? Have you ever seen a tree without leaves?
    b. In spring and summer, the leaves are soft and green. In the fall, or autumn, the leaves start to change colors. What colors might we see? As wintertime gets closer, the leaves turn darker, get weak, and fall off the tree.
    c. Some trees drop their leaves to the ground because they are getting ready to rest for the winter. Other trees, like pine trees (Christmas trees) and palm trees, don't drop their leaves.

3. Look through the **book about trees** and talk about how plants have many different kinds of leaves. Some are big, like maple leaves. Some are very small and sharp, like pine needles. Some are large and fanned, like palm fronds. Talk about the other kinds of leaves the children see in the book.

4. Show the class the tree trunk you have drawn on butcher paper and have the children place the leaves on the tree for the different seasons. As you talk about how leaves grow on trees in the spring, have them take turns taping the green leaves onto the branches of the tree. Discuss how the leaves continue to bloom on trees through the summer (adding more green leaves) and then change colors in the fall. (Either take down the green leaves and tape the colored leaves up, or tape the colored leaves over the green leaves.) Finally, discuss how all of the leaves fall from the trees before the winter comes. (Allow the children to pull all of the leaves off of the trees and scatter them all over the floor.)

5. Toss the leaves into the air and allow them to settle around the room. The more you have, the better! Have the children rake up the leaves. (You can use a real **garden rake** [make sure it doesn't have splinters or sharp metal], a plastic toy, or anything else you have around.) Depending on how many rakes you have, let the children take turns. Show the children how leaves must be raked into a pile. It takes hard work to get all the leaves into the pile. Place several **pillows or blankets** on the floor, and encourage them to rake the leaves into a pile over the pillows and blankets, creating what will look (and feel) like a larger pile. After they have raked the leaves, let the children play with the leaves and pretend to jump in the pile of leaves.

Hands-on Activity: Leaves on the Tree

Skills: creativity, fine motor

1. Before the activity, cut out **brown paper** in the shape of a tree trunk and glue it to a sheet of **white paper**, leaving plenty of room at the top of the paper. Make one for each child.

2. Explain to the children that the **gold glitter** represents sunshine. Sprinkle some over their papers and demonstrate that the glitter just slides right off. Ask them, "What would happen if we added some leaves to this tree?"

3. Show the children how to tear the **construction paper** and **glue** it onto their white papers to make leaves for their bare trees. They can tear many different colors and shapes. See if they can fill up the tree (and also glue properly).

4. Add a little glue to the top of each leaf. Try sprinkling "sunshine" (gold glitter) on the tree again and watch how the leaves catch the sunshine.

Lesson 30 Outing and Parental Supplement

Outing: Leaf Hunt

Skills: curiosity, gross motor, sensory development, social-emotional development

Go on a leaf hunt or nature walk. Bring some paper, writing utensils, crayons, and bags (to collect leaves in). After the children have finished collecting leaves, pull out the paper and crayons and practice tracing, coloring over, or outlining the leaves. Allow the children to do as much or little as they are interested in. Take advantage of the opportunity to move around outside!

Parental Supplement

Books:

- *The Little Yellow Leaf* by Carin Berger
- *Leaf Man* by Lois Ehlert
- *Red Leaf, Yellow Leaf* by Lois Ehlert
- *Leaves* by David Ezra Stein

Activities:

- Put leaves under a piece of paper. Color over the paper to get a leaf print.
- Make a treat for birds using the recipe from the end of *Red Leaf, Yellow Leaf* by Lois Ehlert.
- What kinds of trees and leaves are around your home? Gather some up and try a variety of sorting or counting games.

Discussion:

- Talk about the season you are currently in and what the leaves are doing. What will happen to the leaves next?
- Why do trees need leaves? Why do some trees need bigger or smaller leaves than others?

Unit 5: Things That Grow
Lesson 31: Trees

Lesson Objective: Learn to appreciate trees and all of the things they provide for us.

Lesson 31 Skill Objectives:

- Attention span
- Curiosity
- Fine motor
- Following directions
- Gross motor
- Initiative
- Patience
- Resourcefulness
- Responsibility
- Sensory development
- Social-emotional development
- Taking turns
- Visual tracking

Preparation

Transition Activity Materials:

- Walking rope

Lesson Materials:

- Picnic blanket
- Small box to hold your tree treasures
- Small stick
- Pencil
- Leaf
- Sliced apple or orange
- Syrup in a small cup
- Small pieces of bread or plastic spoons
- Piece of paper

Hands-on Activity Materials:

- Piece of fruit for each child (optional)
- Small container of syrup for each child (optional)
- Piece of paper for each child (optional)

Parental Responsibility:

- Small box from home to hold tree treasures

Lesson 31 Outline

1. Welcome music/gather to carpets

2. Welcome song: "The More We Get Together"

3. Attention grabber: Hocus Pocus, Everybody Focus!
   Skill: following directions, visual tracking

4. Calendar time
   Skills: patience, taking turns

5. Story time: *The Giving Tree* by Shel Silverstein
   Skill: attention span

6. Transition activity: Take a Walk Outside
   Skills: following directions, gross motor

7. Lesson: Trees
   Skills: curiosity, resourcefulness, sensory development

8. Hands-on activity: Treasure Boxes
   Skills: curiosity, gross motor, initiative, responsibility

9. Theme song

10. Children dismissed for free play

Lesson 31 Details

Teacher Tip: Repeat Building Blocks

As we near the end of this curriculum, keep in mind that repetition isn't only intentional—it's essential. For example, the curriculum has children practice certain skills repeatedly, and it consistently, intentionally emphasizes movement, exploration, curiosity, and imaginative play. Just like adults, the more children practice, the more they learn. Seek to see the vision and the value in repeating these essential building blocks of healthy child development!

Transition Activity: Take a Walk Outside

Skills: following directions, gross motor

Weather permitting, hold today's lesson and activity outside. Use your **walking rope** to take a walk outside, reminding the children the importance of holding on to it and staying together. For a fun twist, have the children follow you as you walk, jog, march, skip, or hop to your destination. Have them take turns being the leader. In case of bad weather, use the walking rope to take a walk around your house. Imagine what you would be seeing if you were outside. Pretend to climb a tree, sit in the shade of a tree, or identify different types of trees.

Lesson: Trees

Skills: curiosity, resourcefulness, sensory development

1. Find a nearby tree under which you can sit on a **blanket** and enjoy your lesson and activity. If weather does not allow for this lesson to be taught outside, gather all of the samples ahead of time, and use your imagination as you sit on your picnic blanket indoors and look over all of your tree treasures.

2. Talk to the children about how nice it is to be outside. Ask them to notice some of the beautiful parts of nature that are all around us. Ask, "What are some of the things that we have learned about during this unit that you can see?" (Grass, leaves, etc.) Draw their attention to the tree you are all sitting under. Explain to them that today you will learn about trees and their many gifts to us.

3. Begin by exploring trees using your senses. Ask, "What do trees look like? What sounds do you hear from trees?" (Rustling in the wind, etc.) "What do trees smell like? How do they feel?" Take turns feeling pieces of the bark or leaves.

4. Ask, "Do you know what we have that comes from trees?" Allow them to guess. Display the contents of your **treasure box**, and have them take turns picking things out of the treasure box as you talk about each item. Relate each item to what you can see on or around your tree(s)! (Not all points listed below will correspond to an item in the treasure box.) Go over several or all of the following together:
   a. Trees give us shade (no corresponding item in the treasure box). Ask the children to look up and notice how the tree can shade us from the sun. It can be relaxing to sit or lie in the shade of a tree.
   b. Trees give us beauty (no corresponding item in the treasure box). Ask them to imagine what your yard/area would look like without trees to make it beautiful.
   c. Trees give us branches (represented by the **small stick**).
      i. Ask them to look for branches that have fallen to the ground. If appropriate, break a few branches off for them to look at. (Safety note: To ensure that no one gets scraped or poked, ensure that the children do not run with or swing branches.)
      ii. Ask, "What can we do with branches? We can use them to start fires to help us stay warm." Gather piles of branches and act as though you are building a fire together, warming up together, or roasting s'mores. You can also discuss how birds use branches to make nests.
   d. Trees give us wood (represented by the **pencil**). All trees are made of wood. What can we do with wood? We can build houses, buildings, treasure boxes, pencils, desks, beds, and furniture out of wood.
   e. Trees give us **leaves**. What can we do with leaves? Leaves look beautiful in the trees and on the ground. Last week, we learned more about leaves. What can you remember? Leaves are also the part of the tree that shades us from the sun.
   f. Trees give us fruit (represented by **sliced apple or orange**). Did you know that a lot of the fruit we eat comes from trees? Name all of the fruits you can think of, and talk about which ones grow on trees. Pass out the fruit slices and munch on them together while you talk. Optional: Pretend to pick the fruit out of the trees together before eating them. Or, if you are actually sitting under a fruit tree, eat the fruit from your actual tree.
   g. Trees give us syrup (represented by **syrup in a small cup**). Ask who loves pancakes, and let each child taste the maple syrup by dipping **small pieces of bread** in it or serving it on **plastic spoons**.
   h. Trees give us **paper**. Show the children a piece of paper and talk about how paper is made from trees.

Hands-on Activity: Treasure Boxes

Skills: creativity, fine motor

Tell the children they are going to go on their own treasure hunt and place their "tree treasures" in **their own treasure boxes** to take home. Let them roam around the area, gathering twigs, sticks, leaves, acorns, and bark. (You can also provide them with a **piece of fruit**, a **small container of syrup**, or a **piece of paper**.) Have them sit on the blanket again and show each other what they found. Encourage them to also teach their family members about their tree treasures when they get home.

Optional: If weather does not allow for you to be outside, gather the materials ahead of time, and let the children find the tree treasures inside the house.

Lesson 31 Outing and Parental Supplement

Outing: Orchard or Grove

Skills: curiosity, fine motor, gross motor, sensory development, social-emotional development

Ideally, visit an orchard that has fruit you can pick. Pick baskets of fruit together from the trees, and then eat some together. If appropriate, safe, and not too crowded, play hide-and-go-seek in the trees. If you do not have an orchard or grove in your area, go to a park with different types of trees, and make a checklist with a few examples of trees that you will be able to find in your area (similar to the checklists in Lesson 2 and 3 Images). Encourage the children to identify these trees and check them off of their lists.

Parental Supplement

Books:

- *Trees, Leaves and Bark: A Take Along Guide* by Diane Burns (advanced, but comes with activity and experiment ideas)
- *A Tree Is Growing* by Arthur Dorros (advanced)
- *Tell Me, Tree: All about Trees for Kids* by Gail Gibbons
- *We Planted a Tree* by Diane Muldrow
- *Arbor Day* by Rebecca Rissman
- *Meeting Trees* by Scott Russell Sanders
- *The Giving Tree* by Shel Silverstein
- *A Tree Is Nice* by Janice May Udry

Activities:

- Have your child show the family his tree treasure box. Encourage him to teach you what he learned about things that come from trees.
- Gather sticks together and build something in the backyard.
- Have your child help you gather firewood, and build a fire together. Talk about how trees give us wood that we can burn to stay warm. It is also fun to roast food over the fire. Roast hot dogs or s'mores together.
- Go on a walk together and count all of the trees that you see.
- In a safe and appropriate setting, show your child how to climb a tree.

Discussion:

- Point out things in your home and in your daily routine that come from trees. Encourage your child to notice and point them out as well. Make this into an "I spy" game.
- Point out the differences in trees. Why do some look different than others? Which one does your child like the best?

- What are other fun uses for trees that we haven't talked about? (We can climb trees. We can build tree houses. We can hang swings or hammocks from them. We can hang ornaments on trees at Christmastime.)
- Ask your child, "How many years do you think it took that tree to grow that tall?" Discuss together.

Unit 5: Things That Grow
Lesson 32: Flowers

Lesson Objective: Learn about flowers with a hands-on, artistic approach.

Lesson 32 Skill Objectives:

- Attention span
- Creativity
- Curiosity
- Fine motor
- Following directions
- Gross motor
- Imaginative play
- Individuality
- Patience
- Pre-math
- Sensory development
- Social-emotional development
- Taking turns
- Vocabulary

Preparation

Lesson Materials:

- Small bouquet with at least one flower for each child
- Tweezers
- Scissors
- Glue
- Paper
- Crayons
- Real flowers, fake flowers, or pictures of flowers
- Straws
- Antennae from Lesson 10 (optional)
- Powdered sugar or glitter (optional)

Hands-on Activity Materials:

- Several copies of Lesson 32 Images
- Cardstock
- Craft sticks
- Block of green floral foam

Lesson 32 Outline

1. Welcome music/gather to carpets

2. Welcome song: "The More We Get Together"

3. Attention grabber: Hands on Top, That Means Stop!
   Skill: following directions

4. Calendar time
   Skills: patience, taking turns

5. Story time: *The Reason for a Flower* by Ruth Heller
   Skill: attention span

6. Transition activity: Ring around the Rosie
   Skills: gross motor

7. Lesson: Flowers
   Skills: fine motor, gross motor, imaginative play, pre-math, sensory development, vocabulary

8. Hands-on activity: Make a Bouquet
   Skills: gross motor, vocabulary

9. Theme song

10. Children dismissed for free play

Lesson 32 Details

Teacher Tip: Allow Movement

While movement has always been an essential part of this curriculum, this lesson is a great time to re-emphasize the principle that young children learn best when they are allowed to move. While some of these movements may not seem related to flowers directly, the act of moving throughout this lesson will actually aid children's minds in making valuable connections. Embrace opportunities to allow movement!

Transition Activity: Ring around the Rosie

Skills: gross motor

Play Ring around the Rosie until everyone's wiggles are out.

Lesson: Flowers

Skills: fine motor, gross motor, imaginative play, pre-math, sensory development, vocabulary

1. Begin by talking about flowers. Do the children like flowers? Why or why not? Pass around the **small bouquet of flowers** as you discuss the following points:
    a. Flowers are beautiful because of the colors we can see, the wonderful fragrances we can smell, and the soft petals we can touch. Talk about how we use our senses when we explore flowers.
    b. Flowers help plants make more plants by spreading **pollen*. Flowers have bright colors and smells so that birds and bugs are **attracted* to them. Bees need the **nectar* in flowers to make their honey. Flowers are very important!

2. Sit down at a table and distribute the flowers from the bouquet, one flower for each child. Point out and discuss that flowers have "body parts," just like we do. They have a stem, leaves, petals, and sometimes thorns.

3. Allow the children to use **tweezers** to pluck each petal off of the flowers. You could encourage some counting as they do this. When they finish, use **scissors** to cut each flower into sections (stem, leaves, "tops"). Then have the children **glue** the flower pieces on their **pieces of paper** in the correct order/placement.

4. Flowers are plants, so they need roots. However, since these flowers aren't planted in the ground anymore, they don't have roots anymore either. Have the children use **crayons** to draw roots under the flower.

5. Teach the children about pollination by having some flowers around the room. (You can use **real flowers, fake flowers, or pictures of flowers**.) Have the children pretend to be bumblebees by flying around the room and pretending to collect nectar from the flowers with **straws**. Explain that as the bees go from flower to flower, the pollen gets stuck to them and then comes off on other flowers. Optional: Have children wear the **antennae** we made in Lesson 10.
    a. Optional: If you don't mind the mess, dust each flower with **powdered sugar or glitter**. (You want a substance that will be easily spread without staining clothing.) Have the children move from flower to flower, dipping their straws into the sugar and transferring pollen from one place to another. Safety note: Do not have the children suck on the straw, as you do not want them inhaling glitter or powdered sugar.

Hands-on Activity: Make a Bouquet

Skills: gross motor, vocabulary

Before the activity, make **several copies of Lesson 32 Images**. (There should be at least three flowers for each child.) Cut the images out and mount them on **cardstock** and **craft sticks**. Write movements on the back. (Some ideas include walk backwards, do jumping jacks, do summersaults, slither on the ground, make a carpet angel, hop on one foot, skip across the room, jump like a frog, march, gallop, spin in circles, jump across the room, or do sit-ups or pushups.) Place the mounted flower cutouts around the room so they stand straight up (between couch cushions, in vases, between decorations, etc.), so the children can act as though they are "picking" each flower.

Allow the children to take turns "picking" the flowers one by one. As each child picks a flower, look at it together, and decide what type of flower it is. (The children will need you to tell them at first, but as you repeat types of flowers, see if they can remember!) Talk about the unique characteristics of the different types of flowers that help you identify them. After you have identified the type of flower, read the assigned movement written on the back of each flower. Do that movement as a class, and have a child place the flower in a **block of green floral foam** to create a bouquet. Repeat until you have picked all the flowers.

Lesson 32 Outing and Parental Supplement

Outing: Flower Garden or Florist

Skills: curiosity, gross motor, sensory development, social-emotional development

Visit a flower garden or florist shop, and observe the many colors, sizes, and shapes of flowers growing there. If you don't have a local florist, visit a botanical garden or the garden section of your local Walmart, Home Depot, etc.

Parental Supplement

Books:

- *Flower Garden* by Eve Bunting
- *On Meadowview Street* by Henry Cole
- *Planting a Rainbow* by Lois Ehlert
- *The Reason for a Flower* by Ruth Heller
- *The Flower Alphabet Book* by Jerry Pallotta
- *Ava's Poppy* by Marcus Pfister
- *Zinnia's Flower Garden* by Monica Wellington

Activities:

- Place white carnations in water with food coloring. Watch the petals slowly change colors over the course of a few days.
- Practice counting flower petals. Notice how different kinds of flowers have different numbers of petals. What flower can you find with the most petals? Least?
- Make handprint flowers. Draw a green stem on a paper, dip your child's hand in paint, and let her stamp the "flower." You can also paint with flowers by dipping the petals in paint and stamping your paper.
- Make fun food items in the shape of flowers (ex: cookies or sandwiches.).

Discussion:

- Observe the flower you planted a few weeks ago. How has it grown? Can you see the flower yet? Continue to care for it together.
- Talk about how to properly care for cut flowers. (Ex: putting them in a vase, trimming stems, plucking dead petals, etc.).
- What animals like flowers? Why do bees need flowers?
- Some flowers grow "wild" and others are planted and grown for decoration. Talk about the differences. (Ex: If we see flowers in other people's yards, it is not polite to pick them).

Resources Used by the Authors:
- http://www.teachpreschool.org/2012/06/flower-challenge-fine-motor-flower-fun/
- www.clker.com

Unit 5: Things That Grow
Lesson 33: Foods That Grow

Lesson Objective: Help children realize where their food comes from, while also employing some new critical-thinking exercises.

Lesson 33 Skill Objectives:

- Attention span
- Critical thinking
- Following directions
- Gross motor
- Patience
- Responsibility
- Rhyming
- Sensory development
- Social-emotional development
- Taking turns
- Teamwork

Preparation

Lesson Materials:

- Lesson 33 Images mounted on felt
- Bowl
- Flannel board*

*You can use the flannel board from Lesson 29 or simply tape the images to a wall.

Hands-on Activity Materials:

- Potatoes
- Apples
- Carrots
- Raspberries
- Peas in a pod
- Tomatoes on the vine

Lesson 33 Outline

1. Welcome music/gather to carpets

2. Welcome song: "The More We Get Together"

3. Attention grabber: Stand Up! Sit Down.
   Skills: following directions, gross motor

4. Calendar time
   Skills: patience, taking turns

5. Story time: *Up, Down, and Around* by Katherine Ayers
   Skill: attention span

6. Transition activity: *Up, Down, and Around* with Actions
   Skills: following directions, gross motor

7. Lesson: Where Does Our Food Come From?
   Skills: critical thinking, teamwork

8. Hands-on activity: Find Our Food
   Skills: critical thinking, rhyming, sensory development

9. Theme song

10. Children dismissed for free play

Lesson 33 Details

Teacher Tip: Explore

Remember that exploration is a key to growth. This lesson incorporates a lot of sensory learning. Allow the children to see, taste, and touch the foods you are talking about in this lesson. Enjoy being outside, if possible. Enjoy learning through experience!

Transition Activity: *Up, Down, and Around* with Actions

Skills: following directions, gross motor

After the children have sat through the *Up, Down, and Around* once, have them listen closely and do the corresponding actions while you read it aloud again. When you read, "Up!" have them jump up in the air. When you read, "Down!" have them fall down on the ground. When you read, "Around and around!" have them spin in a circle.

Lesson: Where Does Our Food Come From?

Skills: critical thinking, teamwork

1. Review what you read in today's book. Explain, "Much of our food is grown in the ground, on trees, or on plants. But how does it get to us?"

2. Place the cutouts from **Lesson 33 Images (mounted on felt)** in a **bowl** (except the apple on page 1 of Lesson 33 Images). Have the children take turns picking a cutout from the bowl.

3. Have the first child place his cutout on the **flannel board**. Help that child describe what he sees in the cutout and what it represents as far as the process of where our food comes from.

4. Have the next child pick a cutout from the bowl. As a class, decide if this step comes before or after the cutout that is already on the board. (Example: The first child may pick the picture of the shopping cart, representing that we go to the grocery store to buy the apple. The second child may pick the picture of the apple tree. Ask the children, "Which comes first? Does the apple grow on the tree before or after it arrives at the store?")

5. Once a cutout is on the board, hold up the cutout of the apple (page 1) within the context of the picture. (For example, place the apple in the apple tree, in the basket by the apple

tree, in the semitruck, in the shopping cart, or on the kitchen counter, etc. You won't hold up the apple cutout for the picture of the seeds or the picture of planting).

6. Continue taking turns until all of the pictures are in the correct order. Once the sequence is complete, move the apple from one picture to the next, helping the children see the progression from apple seed, to your kitchen, and then to your stomach. For the last picture of the apple core, point out that the seeds can be used to plant a new apple tree.

7. Take all of the pictures down. See if the children can now put them in the right order with minimal help.

Hands-on Activity: Find Our Food

Skills: critical thinking, rhyming, sensory development

1. Before this activity, place the fruits and vegetables outside where the children can pick or pull them as realistically as possible. For example, bury the **potatoes** in a spot of dirt so that the children actually have to dig in the dirt to find them. Place the **apples** on a low branch of a tree, so the children can pretend to pick them. Try to buy **carrots** that still have some stem on them, and bury them so only their stems are showing. Place the **raspberries** on a bush or shrub. Place the **peas in a pod** in a bowl so the children have to break open the pods and discover the peas inside. Buy **tomatoes on the vine**, and place them in a spot where they might appear to be growing. Be creative with your execution.

2. During the lesson, gather everyone to the correct general area for each particular riddle. Read the riddle. Prompt the children where to look as necessary (they may, for example, need direction about digging for potatoes), but let them figure out as much as possible for themselves.

I grow in a place
That is deep in the ground.
You'll have to start digging,
So I can be found!

You learned about trees
In lessons past.
If you look on the tree,
You can pick me at last!

I am orange on bottom,
But you only see green!
My bottom's down under,
If you see what I mean!

I'm red and so juicy,
And oh so "delish"!
On a bush you will find me,
And eat, if you wish!

I grew on a vine,
And was picked very well.
In a bowl now you'll find me
Inside of my shell!

Like peas, I can grow up
Because of a vine.
I'm bright, red, and juicy,

And will taste oh so fine!
3. Gather the fruits and vegetables that you have picked together, and talk about all the yummy foods you can make with them. Answers could include pies, mashed potatoes, vegetable soup, raspberry jam, etc. Optional: Wash and eat some of the fruits and vegetables together!

Lesson 33 Outing and Parental Supplement

Outing: Picnic

Skills: gross motor, responsibility, sensory development, social-emotional development

Have each parent pack a picnic with his or her child. Have the children help prepare a part of the picnic, and then allow each child to present to the group what he contributed. Use as many fresh ingredients as possible in your meal, and talk to the children about what you are eating, how it grew, and where everything comes from. (Some food ideas include fresh fruit salad, a fresh veggie tray, vegetable soup, sandwiches with a lot of fresh veggies on them, green salads, or any kind of dessert made from fruits.) After you are done eating, enjoy the fresh air and sunshine together.

Parental Supplement

Books:

- *Up, Down, and Around* by Katherine Ayers
- *The Enormous Potato* by Aubrey Davis
- *Eating the Alphabet: Fruits and Vegetables from A to Z* by Lois Ehlert
- *Growing Vegetable Soup* by Lois Ehlert (includes a recipe)
- *Vegetable Garden* by Douglas Florian

Activities:

- Make the vegetable soup recipe included in *Growing Vegetable Soup*, or make your own favorite recipe.
- Attend a local farmers' market. Sample fresh foods where possible. Talk together about where each food came from. As you shop, see if your child can remember the other steps about where food comes from.
- Use the produce or fresh food that you bought together. Can them, make pies or jams, or just enjoy them for meals together. Talk about how fresh foods make us feel healthy and strong.
- Ask someone to give you a tour of his or her farm or garden.
- If you have a place to plant a garden, allow your child to help you pick out what seeds to plant, help you plant them, and care for them.
- Pretend to plant a garden in your living room. Let your child decide what he wants to plant. Ask him what his favorites are.
- Buy some seeds and some corresponding fruits or vegetables. Play a guessing game and guess together which seeds grow into which fruits or vegetables.

Discussion:

- At mealtime, have your child guess which foods were grown and which foods weren't. (Ex: Corn grows in gardens, but bread doesn't.) You can also talk about foods that are made from things that grow. (Ex: These chips did not grow, but they were made from corn that grew.)

Resources Used by the Authors:
- www.clker.com

Unit 5: Things That Grow
Lesson 34: You Grow

Lesson Objective: Explore all aspects of growth that the children have experienced throughout the year.

Lesson 34 Skill Objectives:

- Accountability
- Decision making
- Following directions
- Gratitude
- Gross motor
- Memory
- Responsibility
- Self-awareness
- Self-esteem
- Social-emotional development

Preparation

Lesson Materials:

- Measuring tape or board from Lesson 1
- Mirror
- Children's photos from Lesson 1

Hands-on Activity Materials:

- LMG SUGGESTED SONG LIST
- Party food, games, and decorations of your choice
- Invite all of the parents to attend the class party

Lesson 34 Outline

1. Welcome music/gather to carpets

2. Welcome song: "The More We Get Together"

3. Attention grabber: Do What I'm Doing
   Skills: following directions, gross motor

4. Transition activity: Pick Your Favorite
   Skills: decision making, memory

5. Lesson: Look How We've Grown
   Skills: accountability, gratitude, gross motor, self-awareness, self-esteem, responsibility

6. Hands-on activity: Party to Celebrate You
   Skills: social-emotional development

7. Theme song

Lesson 34 Details

Teacher Tip: Celebrate

Congratulations on completing a successful year! Today, focus on celebrating the children and the great year you had learning together.

Transition Activity: Pick Your Favorite

Skills: decision making, memory

Have the children think back on all of the activities we have done throughout the year. Let them pick one that they would like to do again! If they have trouble remembering, give them some options (ex: leapfrog, I Spy…, Simon Says, dancing).

Lesson: Look How We've Grown

Skills: accountability, gratitude, gross motor, self-awareness, self-esteem, responsibility

1. Ask the children what "growing" means to them. Review some of the things you have learned from Unit 5. Make sure to ask them about the flowers they planted! Have they taken good care of them? Have they seen them start to grow?

2. Briefly review each unit by drawing the children's attention to the fact that each unit ended by discussing them. (Ex: "Remember when we talked about all of the things that are alive? What are some that you can remember? Do you remember that we also talked about how *you* are alive?" Do the same as you discuss each unit.) End the discussion by drawing the children's attention to the fact that *they* grow, just as all of the living things that we have learned about in this unit grow.

3. Teach them that growth for children can occur in more ways than one. Discuss the following ways that the children have grown throughout the year.

4. We grew TALLER! (Just like plants and trees do!) Have you grown taller this year?
    a. Get out the **measuring tape or board from Lesson 1**. Re-measure each child. Show the children the differences in the markings and how much taller they all are than at the beginning of the year.

5. We grew OLDER! As we grow older, our faces change and look a little different each year.
    a. Bring out a **mirror** and the **photos of the children from Lesson 1**.

b. One at a time, hold up a child's photo, and then have her look in the mirror. Allow other children to observe and be involved in each child's process. Ask the children if they can tell a difference. Do they look older than they did at the beginning of the year? How have their faces changed?

6. We grew STRONGER! Have everyone flex their muscles together. Quickly review what you learned in Lesson 13 and Lesson 26 about muscles. (The more we use them, the stronger they become.) You've had an entire year to use your muscles! What can you do with your muscles now that you couldn't do at the beginning of the year? How are you stronger?)

7. We grew FASTER! Because we have muscles in our legs that also grow each time we move, we can move faster and better than we did a year ago! We've learned so much this year about the importance of moving our bodies. The more we move, the faster and stronger we become! Let's practice!

8. We grew WISER! Unlike plants and trees, we have minds that can grow in knowledge! What have you learned this year? What do you understand now that you didn't know when we started?

9. We grew HAPPIER! As we learn to see and appreciate all of the beauties around us and within us, we grow happier! What are some of the beautiful things we have learned about that make you happy?

Hands-on Activity: Party to Celebrate You

Skills: social-emotional development

Start off your party by singing and dancing to "If You're Happy and You Know It" (#3 on the **LMG SUGGESTED SONG LIST**). Throw a party with **food, games, and decorations of your choice.** Invite all of the **parents**, and celebrate a fun and fulfilling year together!

Appendix A: Attention Grabbers

One, Two, Three, Now Follow Me!
Clap a simple sequence of your choice. Have the children copy it.
(Lessons 1, 8, 11, 15, 20, 24, 30)

Do What I'm Doing
Always start with hands on face. Without saying a word, wait for the children to notice and copy what you are doing. Slowly progress through any of the following, expecting them to also follow:
- Open mouth wide
- Do jazz hands
- Stick out tongue
- Pretend to knock on a door (with sound effects)
- Stretch
- Blink three times
- Touch nose
- Fold hands in lap

(Lessons 5, 12, 17, 21, 29, 34)

Hocus Pocus, Everybody Focus!
Move a "magic wand" (a pencil, spoon, dowel, or finger, etc.) through the air like a magician. Have the children track the movement with their eyes.
(Lessons 2, 3, 10, 16, 22, 31)

Hands on Top, That Means Stop!
Place your hands on your head while you say, "Hands on top, that means stop!" You may need to repeat this a few times until all the students copy your movement and you have their attention.
(Lessons 4, 9, 14, 19, 23, 28, 32)

Stand Up! Sit Down.
Have the children copy you as you stand up and then sit down. Repeat this until they have worked out their wiggles and you have their attention.

(Lessons 6, 7, 13, 18, 25, 33)

Appendix B: Free Play Ideas

Blocks
Use any size and style of blocks. Remember that children can learn from building individually as well as from playing together as a group.

Coloring or Drawing
Offer a variety of paper options (blank, colored, coloring pages) and writing utensils (crayons, colored pencil, markers).

Imagination Challenge
Fill a box with random household items. Allow the children to play without any direction on what they should use these items for. Allow them to strengthen their imaginations as they choose the direction of their play.

Outdoor Free Play
Encourage free play outdoors in a safe and supervised area, fostering an atmosphere for independence and exploration.

Paint with Water
Use water and paintbrushes to "paint" on the sidewalk and walls outside.

Play Dough
Play with play dough using cookie cutters, a rolling pin, pieces of plastic drinking straws, plastic knives, etc.

Pipe Cleaners
Push pipe cleaners into the holes of a strainer, twist and bend them into shapes, or thread them with beads, noodles, cereal, etc.

Play Dress Up or Pretend
Have dress-up clothes and supplies (like an apron, bowls, and mixing spoons) for the children to pretend with.

Sensory Bin

Fill a bin with rice, dry beans, or dry pasta, and let children scoop, dig, measure, or find and bury small toys.

Sidewalk Chalk

Encourage the children to draw and create freely. You can also help them create a simple hopscotch game or try chalk paint.

Sock Snowballs

Roll up socks to become "snowballs" and have a snowball fight or throw the sock snowballs into a basket.

Water Table

Play with a water table using plastic containers, cups, funnels, sponges, etc.; toys that float and toys that sink; food coloring for different-colored water (children can mix colors); ice cubes (can also be with food coloring); or soap to make water bubbly.

Appendix C: Song Lyrics and Sheet Music

Songs Used in Every Lesson

"Come Discover, Come Explore" (Live Move Grow Theme Song)

Blink . . . I'm alive!
Jump . . . On my own!
Reach my fingers up to the sky
To show how tall I've grown!

Come discover, come explore . . .
Things that live, and move, and grow.

Join a pirate-y adventure
Where learning is our treasure,
And curiosity maps
The way we go.

Come discover with me!

"The More We Get Together"

Verse 1:
The more we get together, together, together,
The more we get together, the happier we'll be!
'Cause your friends are my friends, and my friends are your friends,
The more we get together, the happier we'll be!

Verse 2:
The more we get together, together, together,
The more we get together, the happier we'll be!
There's Eli, and Clark, and Carter, and Mason,*
The more we get together, the happier we'll be!

Change lyrics to include the children in your group. If there are more or less than four children in your group, adapt lyrics as necessary.

"Days of the Week Song"
(Sing to the tune of "Oh My Darling, Clementine")

There are seven days,
There are seven days,
There are seven days in a week.
Sunday, Monday,
Tuesday, Wednesday,
Thursday, Friday, Saturday.

(Repeat once)

Live Move Grow Suggested Songlist Order

1. The More We Get Together by The Little Kid Series - Smile A Little
2. Live Move Grow Theme Song - Come Discover Come Explore
3. If You're Happy and You Know It by Go Fish - Party Like a Preschooler
4. ABC Song by Abridge Club - Movin' and Shakin' for Youngsters
5. Five Little Ducks by Ingrid DuMosch - Happy Birthday to a Special Boy
6. Shake My Sillies Out by Raffi - The Singable Songs Collection
7. Bingo by Cedarmont Kids - 100 Singalong Songs for Kids
8. Tippy Toes by Music for Moving - Preschool Action Songs 1
9. We Are the Dinosaurs by Laurie Berkner - Whaddaya Think of That?
10. Wiggy Wiggles Freeze Dance by Hap Palmer - Two Little Sounds Fun With Phonics and Numbers
11. Old McDonald Had a Farm by The Hit Crew Kids - 157 Best Songs and Stories
12. The Animal Hokey Pokey by Jack Hartman - Alphabet Zoo
13. The Itsy Bitsy Spider by The Z Brothers - ABZ's
14. Head, Shoulders, Knees and Toes by Gaynor Ellen - Action Songs & Rhymes
15. London Bridge by Kidsongs - The 100 Greatest Kidsongs Collection
16. The Orchestra by Wee Sing - Wee Sing and Pretend
17. The Wheels on the Bus by Cedarmont Kids - 100 Singalong Songs for Kids
18. Planets Song by Have Fun Teaching - Science Songs
19. Row, Row, Row Your Boat by Dora The Explorer
20. I've Been Working on the Railroad by Larry Groce & Disneyland Sing Along Chorus
21. The Airplane Song by The Laurie Berkner Band - The Best of the Laurie Berkner Band
22. Twinkle, Twinkle Little Star by The Countdown Kids - 150 Fun Songs for Kids
23. Down by the Bay by Raffi - The Singable Songs Collection
24. When We Grow Up by FunkeyMonkeys - Tastes Like Chicken
25. Best Friends Forever by Bryant Oden - The Songdrops Collection 2

Come Discover, Come Explore!

Lesson 2 Images

Sight Nature Walk Checklist

Lesson 3 Images

Lesson 4 Images

Lesson 4 Images

Lesson 4 Images

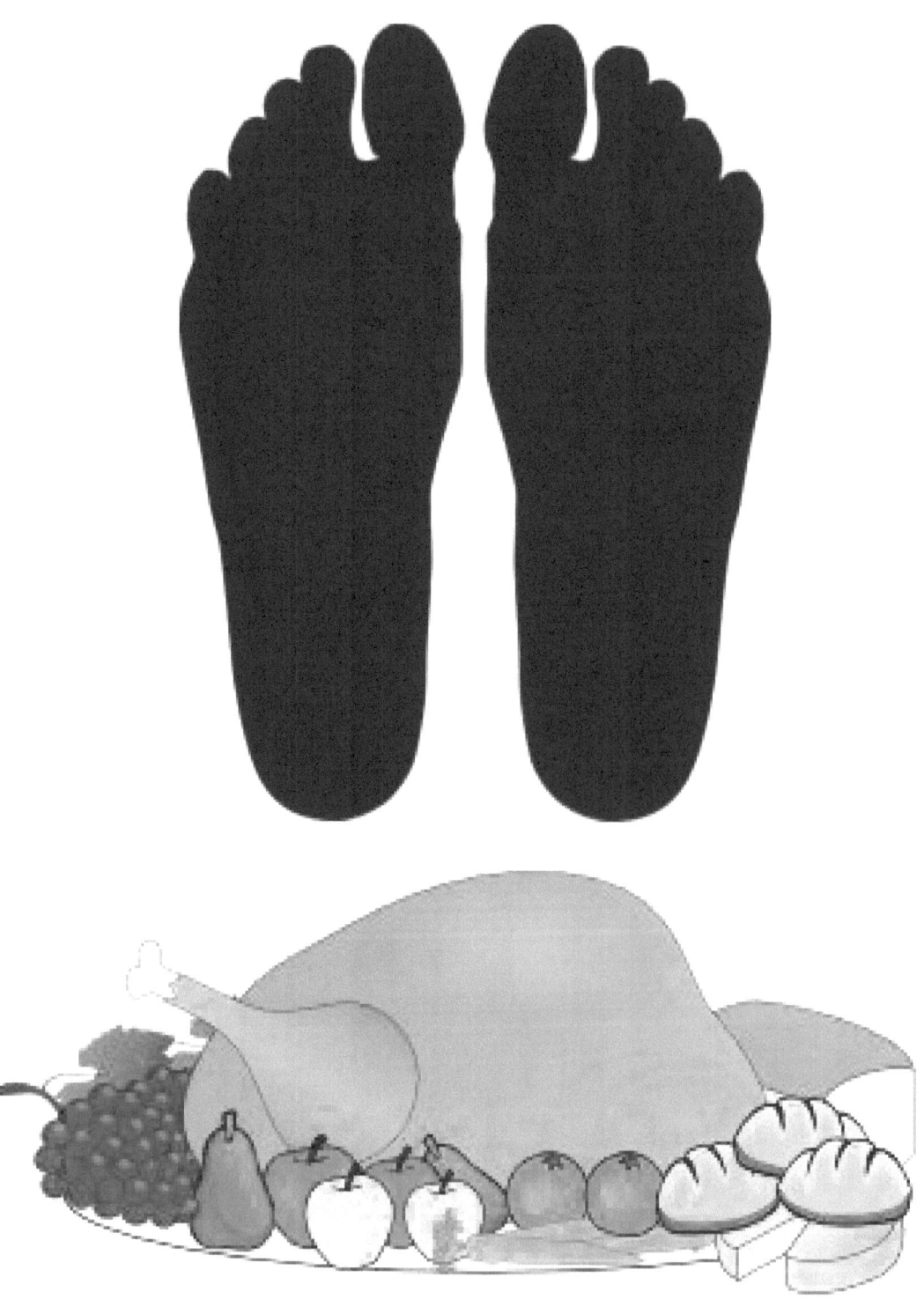

Lesson 5 Images

Lesson 5 Images

3

Lesson 7 Images

Lesson 7 Images

Lesson 9 Images

Lesson 9 Images

Lesson 9 Images

Lesson 10 Images

Alligators[1] eat fish[2] and birds[3] and live in swamps[4].

Crocodiles are "meaner"[1] than alligators, have longer heads[2] than alligators, and like to swim[3].

Snakes eat mice[1] and eggs[2], use their tongue[3] to smell, and slither[4].

Turtles[1] eat grass[2], have shells[3], and lay eggs[4].

Frogs eat insects[1] with their long tongues[2], jump on lilypads[3], and were tadpoles[4].

Lizards eat plants[1] or insects[2]. Some types of lizards are geckos[3] and iguanas[4].

Lesson 12 Images

Turkey beak: yellow
Turkey wattle: red

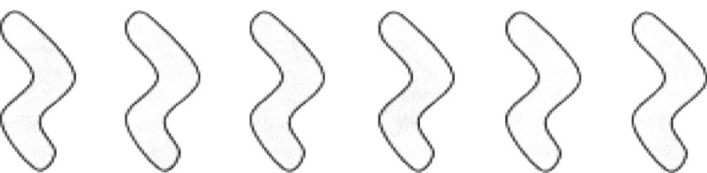

ALL ABOUT ME!

Hello! My name is _____.

This book is all about me!

I am alive! This means I have to feed my body by eating food.

One of my favorite foods to eat is _____.

Because living things need rest too, I go to sleep every night in my home. I sleep in my _____, and I never go to sleep without _____.

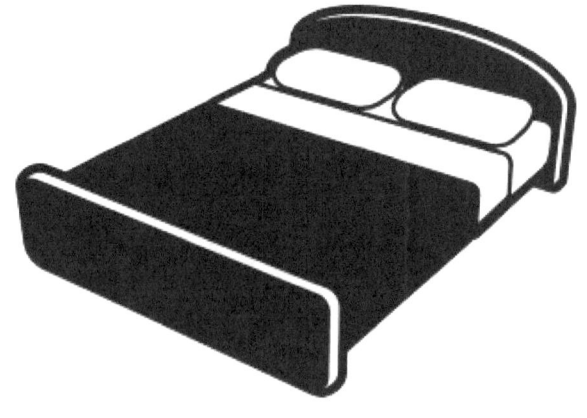

Because I am alive, I know how to talk! My favorite people to talk to are _____.

We like to talk about _____.

My body is amazing! It can do so many things.

My favorite part of my body is _____ because I can _____.

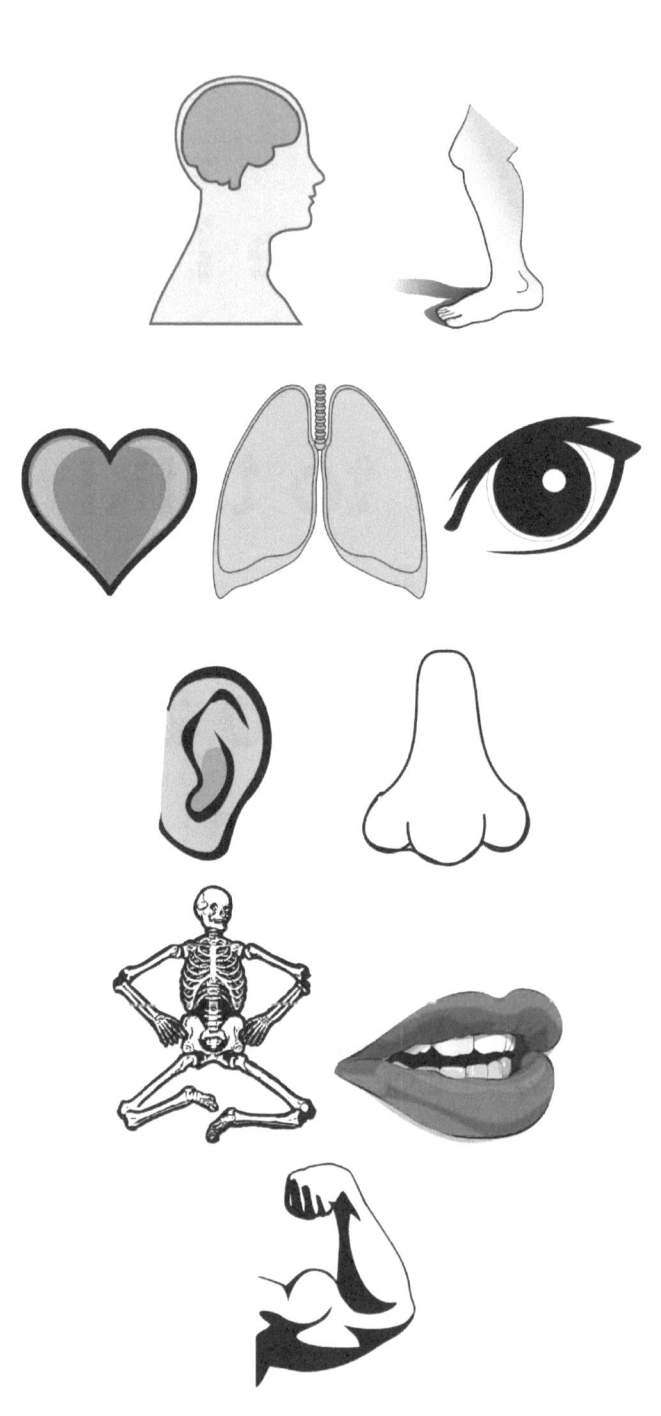

My body is unique, just like me. One of my favorite things about me is _____.

I am unique! I am special! I am me!

clker.com

clker.com

Lesson 19 Images

Lesson 20 Images

Lesson 20 Images

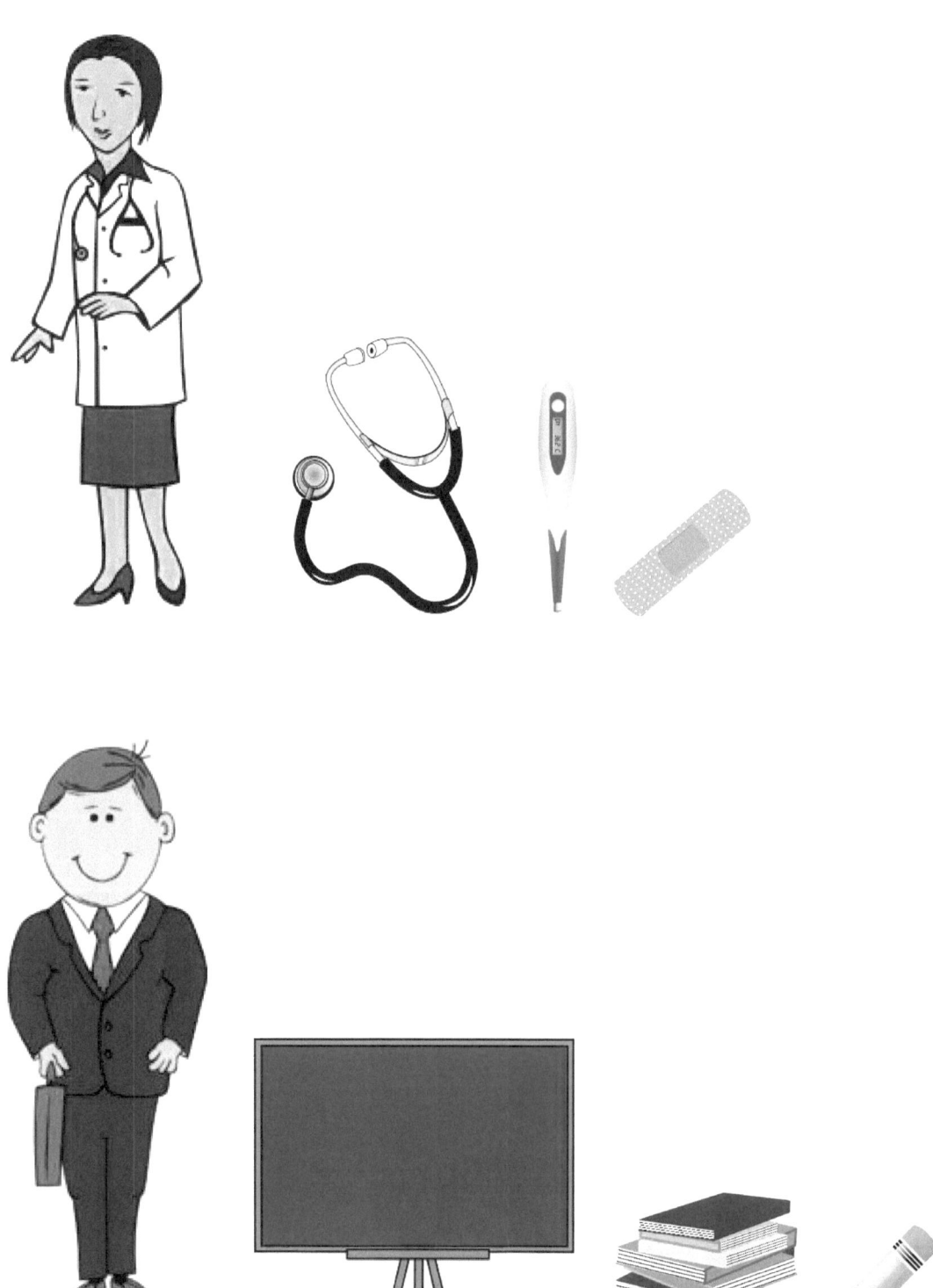

Lesson 20 Images

Lesson 20 Images

Lesson 20 Images

5

When I grow up, I want to be a(n) _____.

I will help others by _____ _____

I will use _____.

My _____ is a _____. _____

My _____ is a _____. _____

Lesson 20 Images

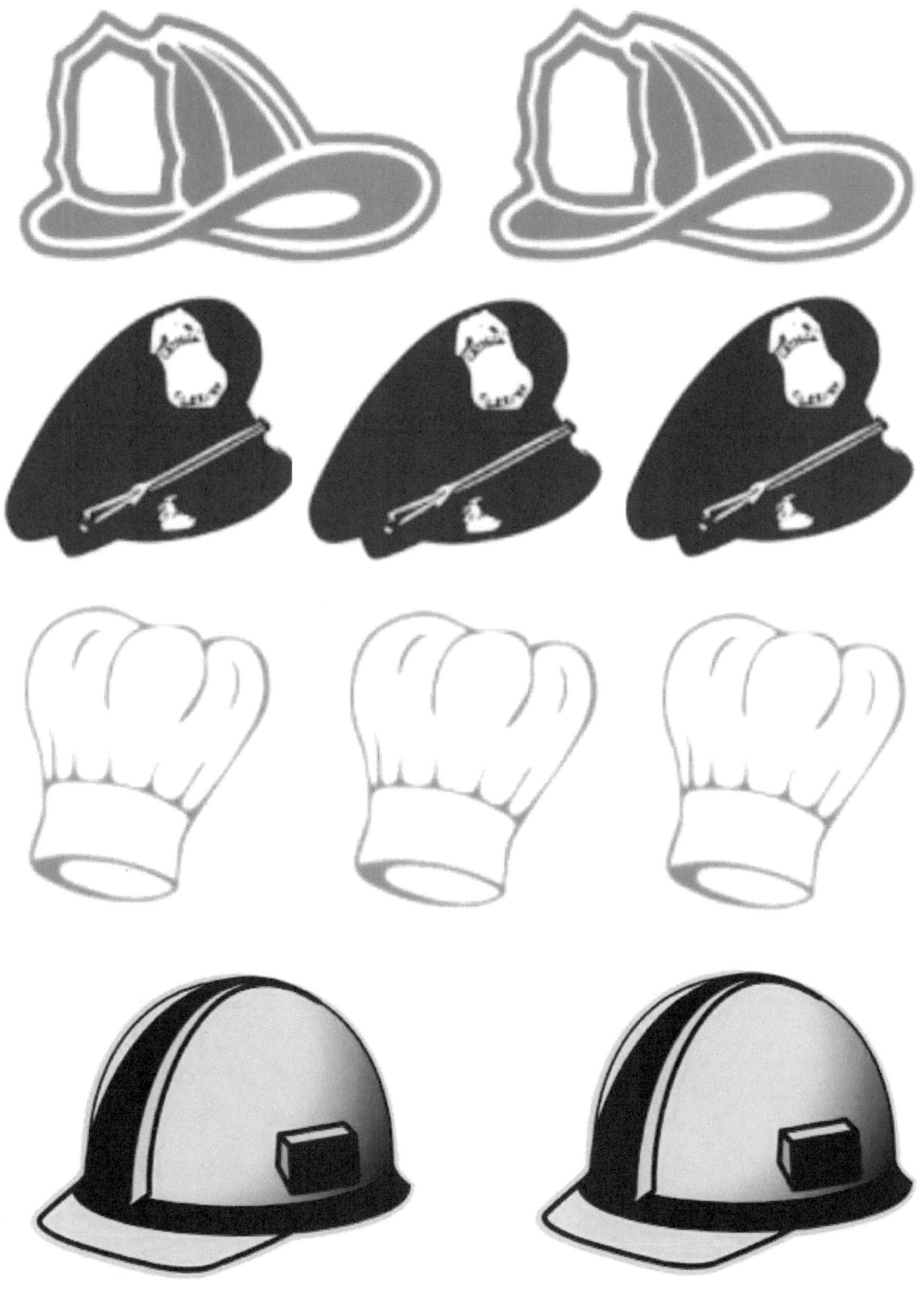

7

Lesson 21 Images

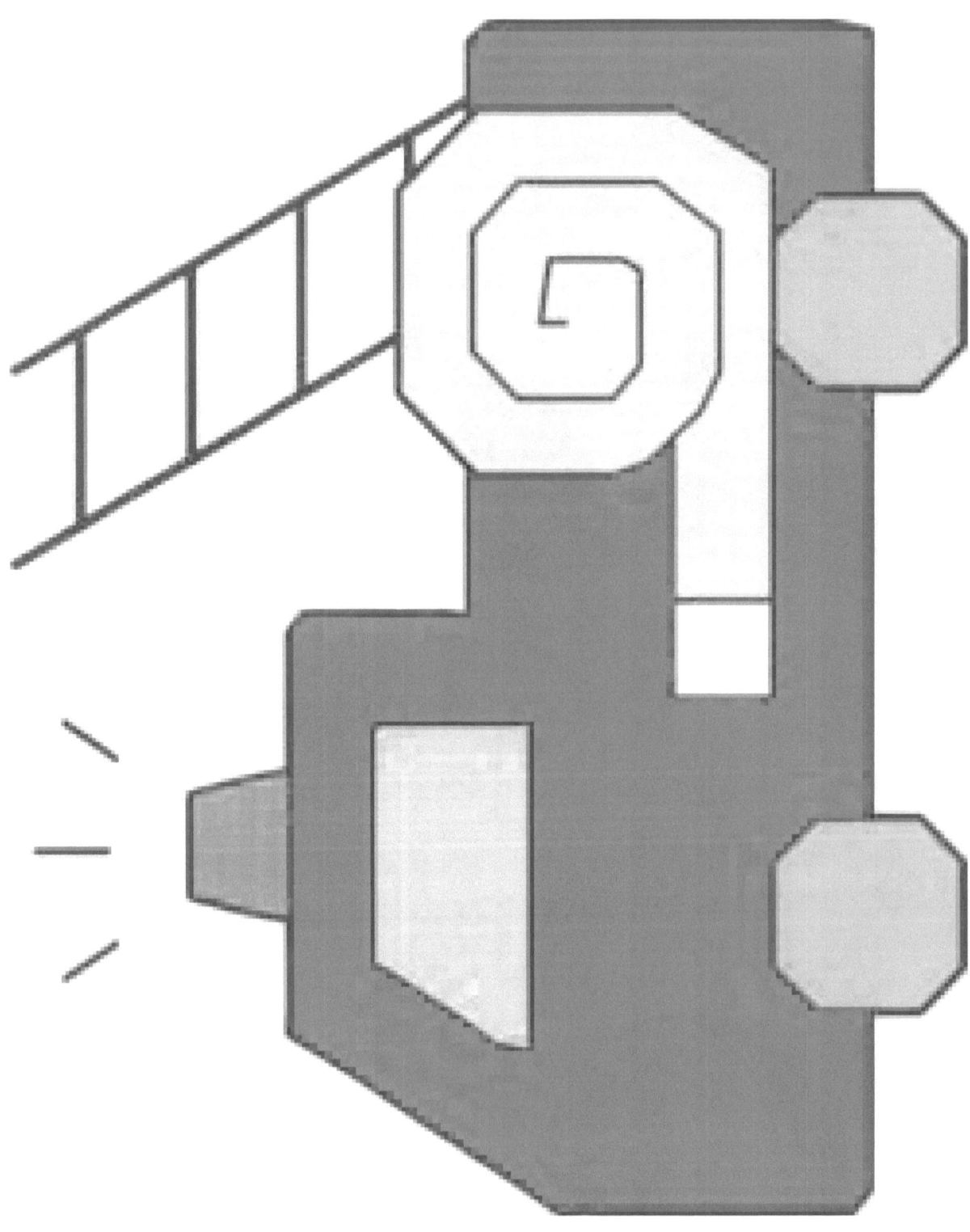

Lesson 21 Images

Lesson 21 Images

Lesson 21 Images

Lesson 21 Images

Lesson 21 Images

Lesson 25 Images

Lesson 28 Images

Lesson 29 Images

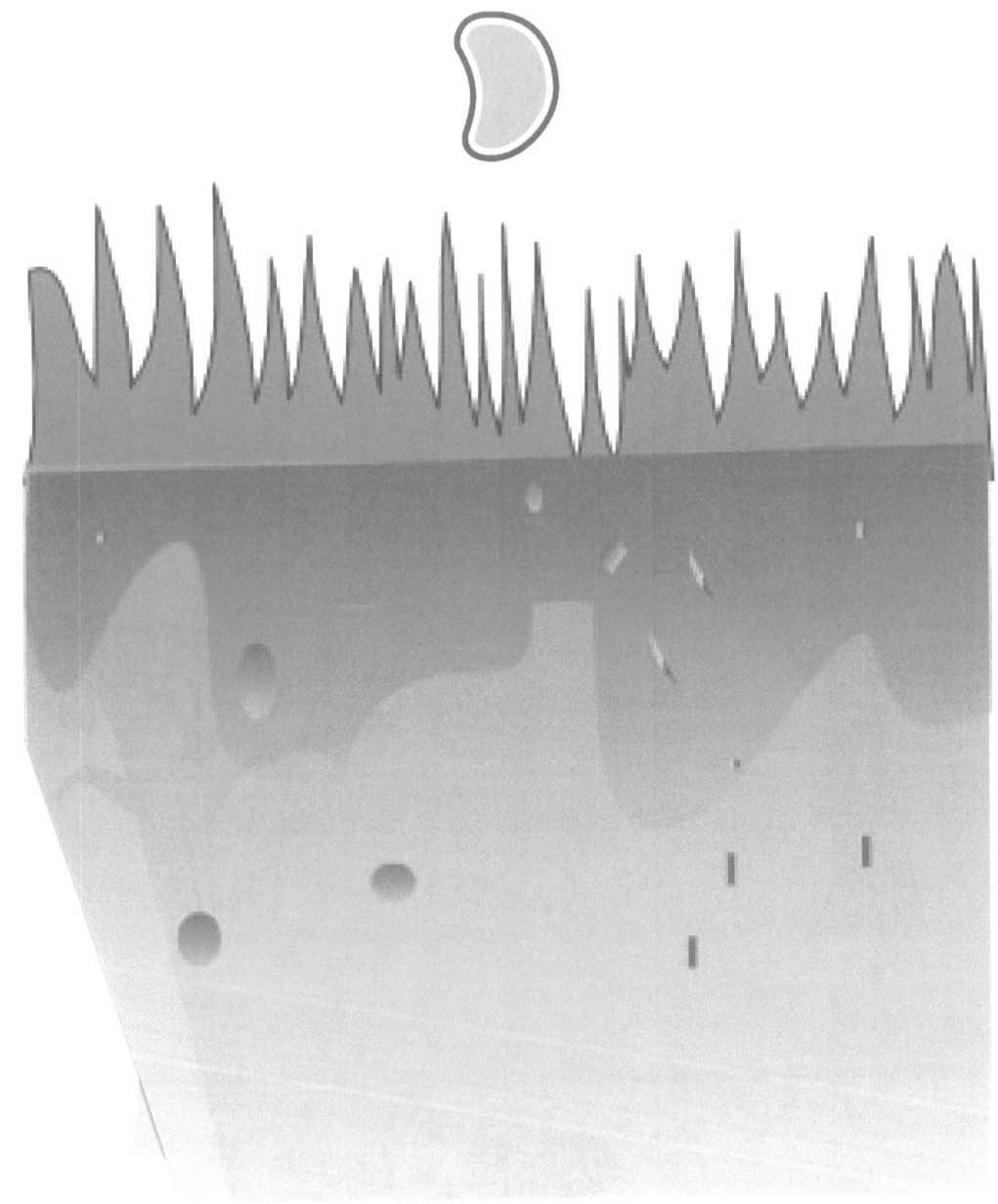

Lesson 29 Images

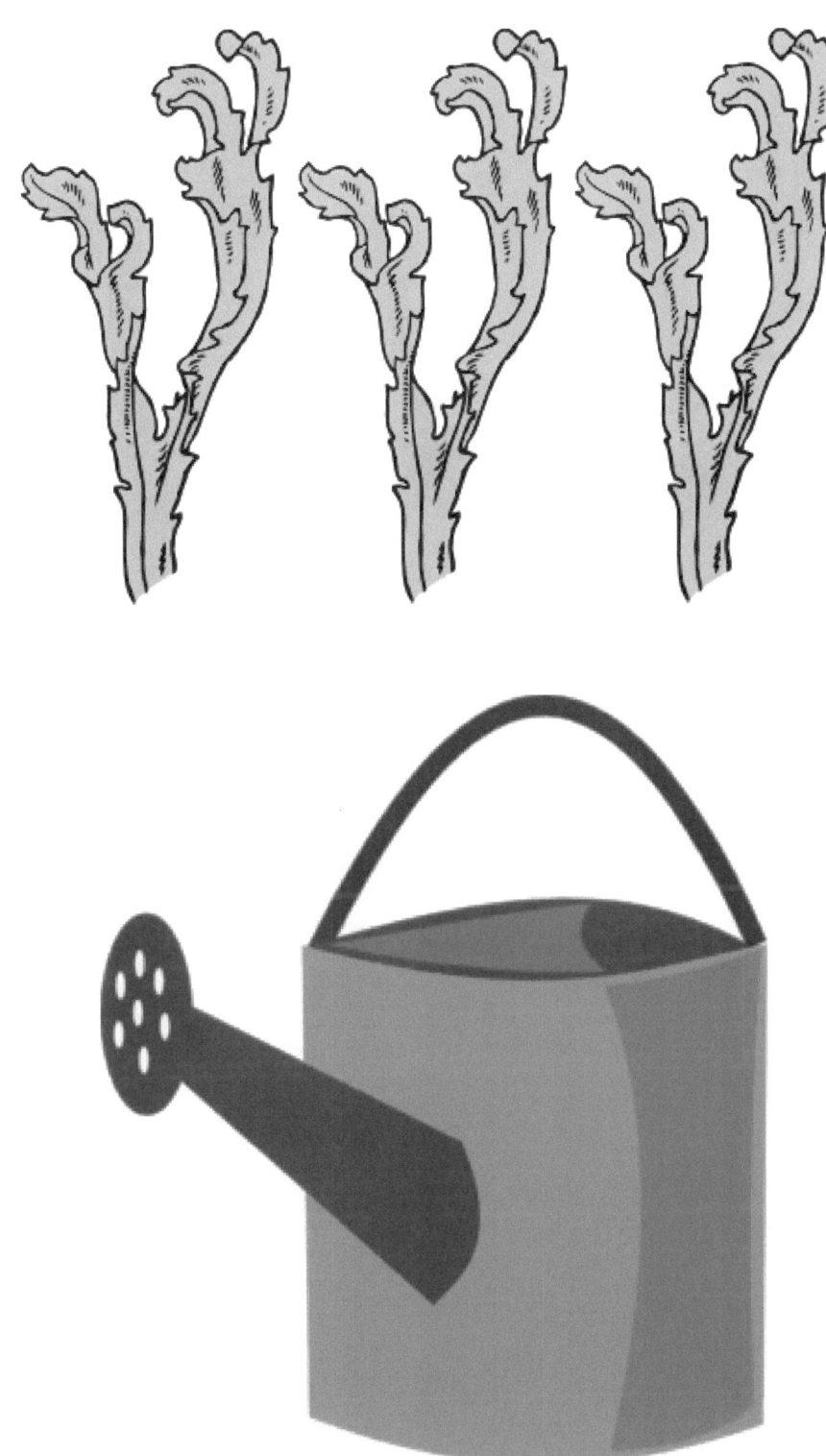

Lesson 29 Images

Lesson 32 Images

ROSE   SUNFLOWER

DAFFODIL   TULIP

Lesson 32 Images

DAISY

LILY

Lesson 33 Images

Lesson 33 Images

Lesson 33 Images

Lesson 33 Images

4

Lesson 33 Images

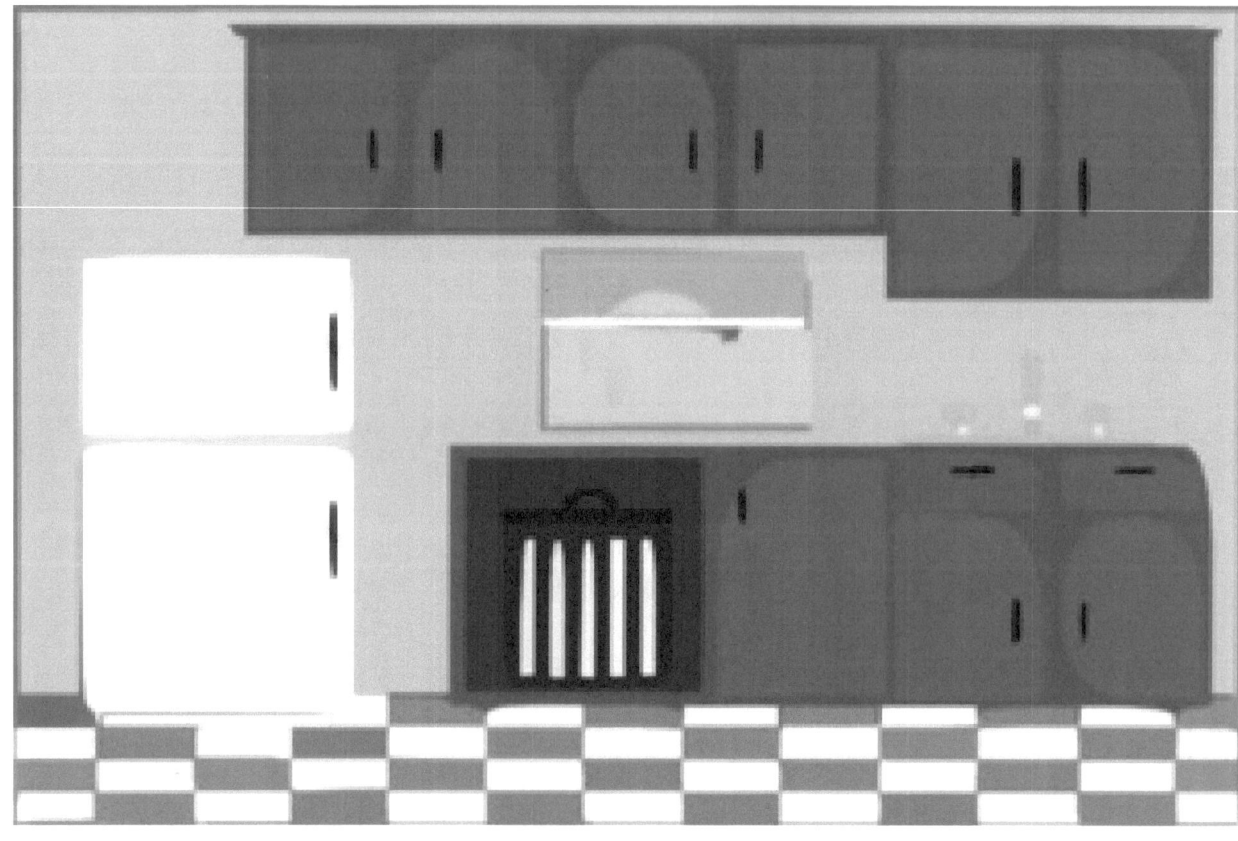

Made in United States
Troutdale, OR
07/30/2024

21646969R00166